# PrestaShop 1.5 Beginner's Guide

Build your own attractive online store with this fast and flexible e-commerce solution

**Jose A. Tizon**

**John Horton**

BIRMINGHAM - MUMBAI

# PrestaShop 1.5 Beginner's Guide

First published: June 2010

Second Edition: April 2013

Production Reference: 1120413

Published by Packt Publishing Ltd.
Livery Place
35 Livery Street
Birmingham B3 2PB, UK.

ISBN 978-1-78216-106-6

www.packtpub.com

Cover Image by Asher Wishkerman (wishkerman@hotmail.com)

# Credits

**Authors**

Jose A. Tizon

John Horton

**Reviewers**

Bart Sallé

Bryan Shaw

**Acquisition Editor**

Andrew Duckworth

**Lead Technical Editor**

Susmita Panda

**Technical Editors**

Saumya Kunder

Ishita Malhi

**Project Coordinator**

Anugya Khurana

**Proofreader**

Samantha Lyon

**Indexer**

Tejal R. Soni

**Production Coordinator**

Pooja Chiplunkar

**Cover Work**

Pooja Chiplunkar

# About the Authors

**Jose A. Tizon** studied computer engineering at the University of Huelva and Czech Technical University in Prague.

He started developing websites as a hobby in the year 2000. It then became a profession, as he is now a Software Development Engineer at Amazon.

In this way, he has developed e-commerce websites for small and big companies in Spain, Czech Republic, and the UK, finding a new experience in every single one.

Jose spends his spare time with his love, Yolanda, and in developing new ideas.

Yolanda, for standing me every day and not getting angry when I spend so much time developing some of my ideas. I love you! Mua.

My parents Antonio and Paqui; brother, Francisco; and my dog, Simba who give me all the support in the world and inspire me.

Ivan (Kaly), for being himself, and friends from Huelva and Prague, who were with me in every significant moment of my life.

Cesar Mariel, for pushing me in the startup world.

The open source community, because without them, this world would be completely different.

And of course, you, for reading this!

**John Horton** is a fan of most things digital and particularly enjoys the growing mobile industry. He has published books, apps, and websites.

He spends his working hours helping people make a success out of their web/ e-commerce enterprises through his design business, www.HadronWebDesign.com.

He is encouraging the pursuit of mathematics through the free Android app, MathLegends. www.MathLegends.com.

In his spare time, he likes shooting Zombies with his two sons.

To the other author, who must take the credit for this book!

# About the Reviewers

**Bart Sallé** is a web developer from the Netherlands specializing in HTML5, CSS3, PHP, MySQL, JavaScript, and jQuery.

He loves open source software and works with TYPO3, WordPress, Joomla!, PrestaShop, WooCommerce, osCommerce, and VirtueMart.

Bart Sallé was one of the first people in the Netherlands who started building his webshops using PrestaShop as a base.

He is still as excited about PrestaShop now as he was back when the first stable version of PrestaShop was released.

His company website can be found at `www.os-evolution.com`.

His personal website can be found at `www.bartsalle.nl`.

I would like to acknowledge Jolanda, my wife, and my beautiful kids, Noa and Fenne.

I would also like to acknowledge my mother Lies, and my father Theo, who passed away in January this year.

# www.PacktPub.com

## Support files, eBooks, discount offers and more

You might want to visit www.PacktPub.com for support files and downloads related to your book.

Did you know that Packt offers eBook versions of every book published, with PDF and ePub files available? You can upgrade to the eBook version at www.PacktPub.com and as a print book customer, you are entitled to a discount on the eBook copy. Get in touch with us at service@packtpub.com for more details.

At www.PacktPub.com, you can also read a collection of free technical articles, sign up for a range of free newsletters and receive exclusive discounts and offers on Packt books and eBooks.

http://PacktLib.PacktPub.com

Do you need instant solutions to your IT questions? PacktLib is Packt's online digital book library. Here, you can access, read and search across Packt's entire library of books.

### Why Subscribe?

- ◆ Fully searchable across every book published by Packt
- ◆ Copy and paste, print and bookmark content
- ◆ On demand and accessible via web browser

### Free Access for Packt account holders

If you have an account with Packt at www.PacktPub.com, you can use this to access PacktLib today and view nine entirely free books. Simply use your login credentials for immediate access.

# Table of Contents

# Preface

If you want to start your e-commerce business but are not so much of a technical person, then PrestaShop could be your solution because it is an easy, open source, and free-for-use software that helps sell your products over the Internet.

PrestaShop is a live software, due for an open source license; there is a big community developing new features and fixing bugs very fast.

This book is called a "beginner's guide" only because that is where it starts! Using both realistic and unusual case studies throughout, PrestaShop 1.5 Beginner's Guide will take you on a click-by-click, yet whirlwind journey to the realization of a fully featured, highly professional e-commerce business.

## What this book covers

*Chapter 1*, *Getting Started*, covers how to download and prepare the PrestaShop files, make a database, install PrestaShop, and implement post-installation security.

*Chapter 2*, *Back Office*, helps you with setting the shape of your store, including the logo. We will set up your home page, make some more key pages such as "Contact us" and "Conditions of use", and change and customize themes.

*Chapter 3*, *Merchandising for Success*, discusses and implements an efficient category structure. We will add high quality product descriptions that sell and take a look at all the different ways in which you can use PrestaShop to highlight products. We will also take a look at product features, attributes, accessories, and customization.

*Chapter 4*, *Getting More Customers*, provides information on how to choose the best keywords and provide food for the search engines. We will refine PrestaShop search. We will also cover tag clouds, how to use the PrestaShop CMS, URLs in PrestaShop, robots and site maps, and how to use PrestaShop language features.

*Chapter 5, Tools, Newsletters, Extra Income, and Statistics*, looks at all of the most useful things on the Preferences tab. We will set up a newsletter and notifications system, talk about running an e-mail marketing campaign, set up PrestaShop statistics, and also set up Google Analytics.

*Chapter 6, Security and Disaster Recovery*, looks at the ways in which your shop can be damaged. We will add users, profiles, and permissions to increase security. We will talk about and optionally implement SSL to protect your customers' private information. We will learn how to back up and restore your shop in case everything else fails. We will also talk about upgrading PrestaShop and how this helps keep your business secure.

*Chapter 7, Checkouts and Shipping*, helps us choose and set up a payment provider. We will take a look at alternative payment methods, sales taxes, discuss and implement gift vouchers, and learn how to accept foreign currencies. We will look at the multitude of ways in which to set up shipping options for your customers to choose from, and make sure that they get charged correctly.

*Chapter 8, Ready to Sell*, shows us how to create a customer account and place an order. We will look at the PrestaShop customer loyalty scheme and at how to get some feedback on your products using the PrestaShop Product Comments module. We will tell the search engines about your cool new shop. We will also look at a multi-pronged marketing campaign that includes vouchers and social media. The last thing we will do is cover some functionality of the Customers and Orders tabs that we haven't covered already.

*Chapter 9, Go... to the Future*, we will cover analyzing, optimizing, and adding to your PrestaShop site. We will see "the big secret" and also the future of e-commerce and PrestaShop.

*Appendix A, Control Panel Quick Reference*, briefs you about the tabs and subtabs available in PrestaShop.

*Appendix B, Web Resources*, lists down the web resources to help you build your e-commerce business.

# What you need for this book

Before you get down to building your PrestaShop store, you will need a localhost or a hosting provider to install your own PrestaShop site.

If you already have a web host, here are the system requirements for installing and using PrestaShop. Give your host a call if you are unsure; change if they can't accommodate you. Most good hosts will be fine, as the requirements are very "normal":

◆ Linux, Unix, or Windows operating system

◆ Apache web server

◆ PHP 5.1 or later versions

◆ MySQL 5.0 or later versions

Some PHP 5 versions are bugged (like 1&1) and prevent PrestaShop from working correctly. The following is a list of PHP versions that you should avoid installing for PrestaShop:

◆ PHP 5.2.1 (authentication is impossible)

◆ PHP 5.2.6 (authentication is impossible under 64-bit servers)

◆ PHP 5.2.9 (image management/upload broken)

◆ PHP < 5.2 (invalid date-time zone)

# Who this book is for

This book is for anybody who wants to build a fully functional, real e-commerce store using PrestaShop. You do not have to have any previous knowledge of PrestaShop or any aspect of e-commerce or business in general. If you do, then you will probably find this guide really valuable as well. The book covers all you need to know, but you must just bring the desire to have your own e-commerce business.

# Conventions

In this book, you will find several headings appearing frequently.

To give clear instructions of how to complete a procedure or task, we use:

## Time for action – heading

1. Action 1
2. Action 2
3. Action 3

Instructions often need some extra explanation so that they make sense, so they are followed with:

## What just happened?

This heading explains the working of tasks or instructions that you have just completed.

You will also find some other learning aids in the book, including:

## Pop quiz – heading

These are short multiple-choice questions intended to help you test your own understanding.

## Have a go hero – heading

These are practical challenges that give you ideas for experimenting with what you have learned.

You will also find a number of styles of text that distinguish between different kinds of information. Here are some examples of these styles and an explanation of their meaning.

Code words in text, database table names, folder names, filenames, file extensions, pathnames, dummy URLs, user input, and Twitter handles are shown as follows: "The file that we are going to play with is called global.css. It is in the CSS folder inside our main template folder."

**New terms** and **important words** are shown in bold. Words that you see on the screen, in menus or dialog boxes for example, appear in the text like this: "On the **Select Destination Location** screen, click on **Next** to accept the default destination.".

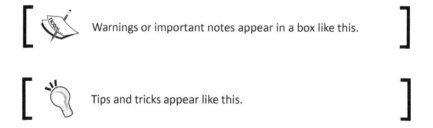

Warnings or important notes appear in a box like this.

Tips and tricks appear like this.

# Reader feedback

Feedback from our readers is always welcome. Let us know what you think about this book—what you liked or may have disliked. Reader feedback is important for us to develop titles that you really get the most out of.

To send us general feedback, simply send an e-mail to feedback@packtpub.com, and mention the book title through the subject of your message.

If there is a topic that you have expertise in and you are interested in either writing or contributing to a book, see our author guide on www.packtpub.com/authors.

# Customer support

Now that you are the proud owner of a Packt book, we have a number of things to help you to get the most from your purchase.

## Errata

Although we have taken every care to ensure the accuracy of our content, mistakes do happen. If you find a mistake in one of our books—maybe a mistake in the text or the code—we would be grateful if you would report this to us. By doing so, you can save other readers from frustration and help us improve subsequent versions of this book. If you find any errata, please report them by visiting http://www.packtpub.com/submit-errata, selecting your book, clicking on the **errata submission form** link, and entering the details of your errata. Once your errata are verified, your submission will be accepted and the errata will be uploaded to our website, or added to any list of existing errata, under the Errata section of that title.

## Piracy

Piracy of copyright material on the Internet is an ongoing problem across all media. At Packt, we take the protection of our copyright and licenses very seriously. If you come across any illegal copies of our works, in any form, on the Internet, please provide us with the location address or website name immediately so that we can pursue a remedy.

Please contact us at copyright@packtpub.com with a link to the suspected pirated material.

We appreciate your help in protecting our authors, and our ability to bring you valuable content.

## Questions

You can contact us at questions@packtpub.com if you are having a problem with any aspect of the book, and we will do our best to address it.

# 1

# Getting Started

*With this book you will be able to set up an e-commerce solution within a week! So are you ready to sell your ideas with PrestaShop?*

In this chapter we will:

- Download and prepare the PrestaShop files
- Make a database
- Install PrestaShop
- Implement post-install security
- Have a look at your shop from a customer's viewpoint
- Have a look around your new admin control panel

Here we go...

## Know your business

Before you start a business, you have to know the product you are selling. If you are not convinced, the buyer themselves may think twice before buying it. Be focused on your chosen market and on your target customers. An example of a great e-commerce solution is www.amazon.com. Amazon, the biggest e-commerce solution in the world, began selling books from a garage with a singular focus on a chosen market and target customer.

# Downloading PrestaShop

Visit www.prestashop.com to get your free copy of PrestaShop. Click on the **Download** option. Select your favorite language and click on the big green button **Download Now**. It is optional whether you fill in the very brief registration information. When you click on the download button you should have a zipped file called prestashop_1.5.x.x.zip, where x.x is the version of PrestaShop you have downloaded. The version number you have doesn't matter. As long as you follow the download link from the PrestaShop home page, you will have the latest stable version.

In the next tutorial, we will upload all the loose unzipped files to your web server. It is worth pointing out that you might save some time by uploading the zipped file and using your web host's file manager to do the unzipping. As most web hosts use a slightly different system, I will guide you through unzipping first. But if you know how to use your web host's file manager to do this, you could save some time while uploading. You decide. Unzip it now to prepare for the next guide and you will be left with a folder called prestashop.

# Technical requirements

To install PrestaShop on a computer, you will need a prepared package. WAMP for Windows, which you can download from www.wampserver.com, or if you are Mac user you could use MAMP, which can be downloaded from www.mamp.info. You can also use XAMPP to install PrestaShop in a different OS and you can download it from www.apachefriends.org/en/xampp.html.

To install PrestaShop on the Internet you will need a domain name, a web server like Apache, Nginx, or Microsoft IIS with PHP 5.1 or higher installed and enabled, and MySQL 5.0 or higher installed with a database created and FTP access.

Now that you have downloaded and unzipped the PrestaShop files, it's time to put them onto your website ready to install. If you are hosting at home, this is a simple matter of putting them in the Apache home folder (see my downloadable guide if you're unsure where this is).

If you are developing on a live server, then you need to transfer the files via FTP. Let's do that step-by-step.

# Time for action – transferring files to your web host

To make this as quick and easy as it can be, I will use a few Windows shortcuts in this short click-by-click guide. Just before you dive in, you will need your FTP username and password. If you don't know it already, you can usually find this quite easily by looking in your account details in your web host's control panel. Any doubts, give them a ring or send an them an email – after all, that's what you pay them for!

1.  Press the *Windows* key and tap the *E* key twice. You will have two Explorer windows pop up. Arrange them neatly one above the other. Alternatively, you can grab a copy of a dedicated FTP program such as FileZilla from `www.sourceforge.net`. There is a small learning curve doing this, but once you're used to it, you will have more options when using FTP. This guide assumes you do not have FileZilla, but if you do, it won't be a problem to interpret the guide.

2.  Browse to the unzipped `prestashop` folder at the bottom of the window and click on it. We do not need the folder itself, just the contents.

3.  At the top window, you need to log into your website via FTP. In the address bar at the top of the screen, type `ftp://yourdomain.xxx` and press *Enter*. When a pop-up window appears, enter your FTP username and password that you obtained earlier.

4.  Now at the bottom of the window, left-click on the very first file. Press the *Shift* key and then, using the down arrow key while still pressing *Shift*, scroll to the very bottom of the screen so that every single file and folder is highlighted.

5.  Now let go of all the keys on the keyboard. Left-click and hold the left mouse button. You can now drag all the files from the `prestashop` folder on your PC up to your website in the top window.

6.  Wait for the files to upload. The time will vary according to the speed of your Internet connection.

## What just happened?

What you have done is put all of the files and folders containing the entire computer code, data, images, and other resources into your web host's server, ready for the next phase of installation.

So let's move on.

# Making a database

PrestaShop needs a MySQL database to function. The files we have just uploaded are the web pages that will become your store and the PHP programming code that performs the actions required by your store.

For example, when a customer creates an account in your new shop, the programming code contained in the files that we uploaded will fill out and store the information in a completely separate computer program. This program is called a database server and the type of database server that PrestaShop uses is called MySQL. Usually, when you are pro-hosting, this server will be an entirely different physical computer to the one holding your files (the web server). As with many servers/computer programs, you need a username and password to access its functions. You also need a unique name for a database for your shop on that server, and you need to know the address locating the server. As an example, this could be `mysql.yourdomain.xxx`. Or it could be something completely different.

Now many web hosts will have already allocated database server details to your hosting account. If this is the case, then you only need to find them and make a note of them for the next phase of the installation.

Most likely your web hosts have a simple two-or three-click process for creating a database. You can then access the details of this newly created database in order to proceed.

Precise details will vary from host to host and also the order in which the options are presented (if at all). The database creation process goes like this.

If you already have a created database, that is okay. PrestaShop can function on a database used by other applications. However, to make sure that they do not conflict, or worse, damage each other, pay close attention to the *How to install PrestaShop* section to be sure of how to create a table prefix!

## Time for action – creating a database

First of all, you need to log in to your hosting control panel. You are looking for an option called **MySQL**, **MySQL databases**, **phpMyAdmin**, or perhaps just **Databases**.

1. Click on **MySQL databases** or something named as **Databases**.
2. Now we need to make another database. Look for the option **Create new**, **Make a database**, or perhaps just **Add**. Click on it to see the options presented. The following is a screenshot of the database creation page on the `DreamHost.com` control panel. It serves as a good example because it has more options than most. If your screen has fewer options, that is okay. Just follow the guide for the bits you need.

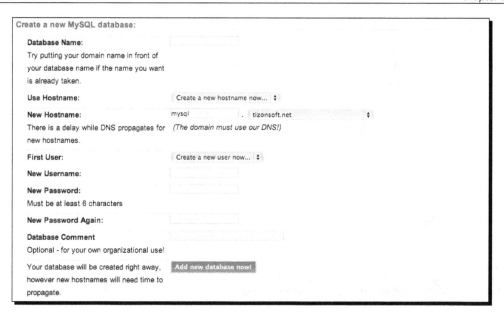

**Database Name** is an important detail that needs to be remembered. It is case sensitive, so upper and lower case must be accurately recorded. Choose a name; again, it is arbitrary, but use something appropriate and not easily guessable, like `mydomainsomesecretnumber`. There will be a maximum number of characters, so you might need to use a shortened version. Write it down or copy and paste it into Windows Notepad or on a similar application. It is possible that you do not have a field for a name or it has already been filled out automatically. That's fine. Just write it down.

3. Enter a memorable but unguessable password. Again this might be decided for you and it might not have this option at all. Re-enter the password if required. Write it down or copy and paste it in the Notepad or something similar.

4. If you get the choice to select versions for MySQL, tick/check the option for 5 or later.

5. If you get the option to **Allow Direct Database Access**, this is a definite **No**. We don't want people to fiddle with our database from far away.

6. When you're done, click to create the database— **OK**, **Finish**, **Create**, **Add new database now**, or whatever your web host decides to label their button with.

7. Now you should be able to see a summary of the database you created. Complete with the values you chose and the values chosen for you. As usual, write it all down or copy and paste it into Notepad or some similar application.

## What just happened?

Now we have a fresh database just itching to be filled up and manipulated. We also have the database information we need to do so. Now we go to the most interesting part of the process and get our very first glimpse of PrestaShop in action. We'll set up the program right away.

# How to install PrestaShop

Now for the fun part, when you get to see some results. What we are going to do is run the PrestaShop auto-installer. This will be a series of web pages where you will enter information to allow the auto-installer to configure your store.

The sort of information that we will be entering is business information such as your shop name, personal details, and of course the database information gathered previously.

## Time for action – the PrestaShop auto-installer

To get started, type your shop domain name into your web browser. It will automatically redirect you to the default start of the PrestaShop installation program. You should then perform the following steps:

1. First, just choose your language and tick on the licenses agreement. Then click on **Next** to move to the **System Compatibility** screen as shown in the following screenshot:

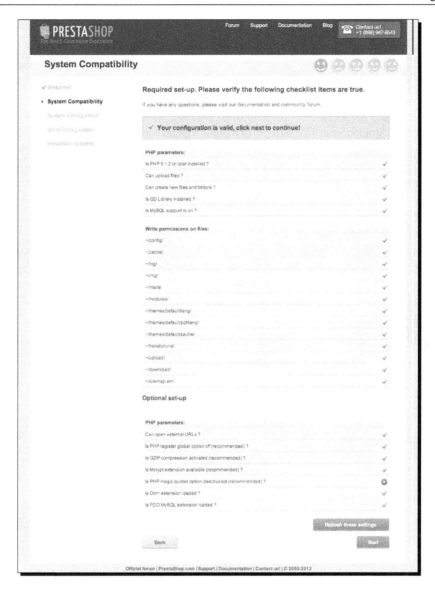

2.  Check that you have all green ticks in **PHP parameters** and **Write permissions on files**, as in the preceding screenshot. On the **Optional set-up** you can have some crosses, but they are not obligatory. If you do, then click on **Next** to proceed and jump to the next step. If you see some scary red crosses, don't panic because there are some simple solutions here. If you have all green ticks move on to step number 6.

**3.** If you have any red crosses under the PHP settings, then you need to contact your web host and ask them to make some changes for you. If your hosting package has the system requirements discussed earlier, it is most unlikely you have any crosses here. Also, if you have installed hosting on your own PC, they will all be ticks. If you have crosses and need to contact your web host, then read the next point first.

**4.** The next is **Write permissions on files**. This is the most likely area to have some crosses and also has the easiest remedy. In order for PrestaShop to install itself, it needs to modify (write to) various files and folders. A red cross indicates that the folder cannot be written to. Changing this is nice and easy. Log in to your website with FTP just as we did when we transferred the PrestaShop folders there. Locate any folders with a red cross, right-click on them, and select **Properties**. Then put a tick in the top two checkboxes under the **Write** column. Done! It is possible that you might need to use your web host's file manager to do this step. Also, if you extracted the files on your web server, then the file permissions will probably not need amending at all. The last optional settings are just that, entirely optional. And again if you are pro-hosting, your web host will need to resolve this for you, but PrestaShop will still be functional without them.

**5.** Click on the **Refresh these settings** button to check if you have solved the problem(s) and then click on **Next** and read on.

**6.** The next is the **System Configuration** screen:

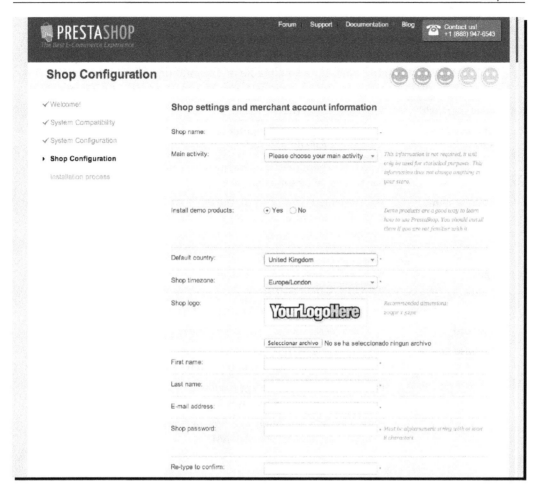

**7.** You might have probably guessed that this is where you will fill in all the database information that we collected earlier. I will go through each setting one at a time because some of the fields are described differently from host to host and by PrestaShop. I feel the need for a small table of explanations. Here it is:

| PrestaShop field | Explanation/alternative name |
|---|---|
| Database server address | This is the address of computer (server) with your database on it: Sometimes called "address", "host name", or just "database server". |
| | Type this in here exactly as it appears in your web hosting control panel. It could be something like `mysql.yourdomain.xxx`. |
| Database name | This is simply a name given to the database on the database server: On shared hosting environments, this is often the same thing as the username (or login as PrestaShop calls it). |
| | Enter exactly as it appears in your hosting control panel. |
| Login | Your MySQL username: On shared hosting environments, this is often the same as database name. |
| | Enter exactly as it appears in your hosting control panel. |
| Password | Your top secret sequence of letters and numbers (Shhh...). |
| Database Engine | This is the way to store your data in your database. You will see a drop-down menu with two options: **InnoDB** and **MyISAM**. |
| | **InnoDB** is the default storage engine for MySQL and **MyISAM** was the default storage engine for MySQL. |
| | Here select **InnoDB**, but if your hosting does not have this option, then you will need to use **MyISAM**. |
| Tables prefix: | This is a short series of letters placed before all the tables (sections) of your soon-to-be-created database. When an e-commerce shop of any type is created, there are dozens of tables created to store all the necessary information. If you think about it, all stores are likely to have similar table names (perhaps "customers" or "products"). When this occurs, adding a unique prefix prevents the new table destroying the old. |
| | A prefix is a good idea at any time, a very good idea if you have any other uses for your database and essential one if you have more than one PrestaShop on your database. |
| | If this is your first PrestaShop, I suggest leaving the prefix as it is, that is `ps_`. But if this is your second or third, I suggest changing it to `ps2_` or `ps3_`. |

Now click on the button **Verify now!** If everything goes smoothly you will see the following message: **Database is connected**. If not, please review all the fields and check it with your hosting provider.

1. Leave the **Configure SMTP manually** box unchecked. This is unnecessary for a pro-hosted environment. Then click on **Next**.

2. Enter your preferred e-mail address on your shop's domain that you would like PrestaShop to use. PrestaShop will send e-mails to customers to thank them for orders, notify them of dispatch, and more. PrestaShop will also contact you to let you know about important events such as when people spend money!

3. Click on **Next** and your shop database will be made. You will see the following screenshot:

4.  This page is really simple but with a little twist. Just fill in your **Shop name** and select the **Main Activity** as you like. As a piece of advice select **Yes** for **Install demo products**. Now select the country where your shop is based and its time zone. You can upload your Shop logo later, but if you want to do it now, you have to upload a 209 x 52 pixel graphic logo from your PC. To log in to your admin control panel use first and the last names along with the email and password. Do not select the **Receive this information by e-mail** checkbox, as we will enable this later. Click on **Next** and rejoice.

## What just happened?

You have just made your first PrestaShop. Cool! A few more bits and pieces to fiddle with and you're done. Was that difficult? In my opinion, if there is a technical side to running a PrestaShop e-commerce business, then that was probably about as geeky and technical as it gets! If you are reading this, you are heading for success.

# Post-install security

Just a few, very quick modifications to your PrestaShop files and it's done.

## Deleting the install folder

What we need to do is delete the entire folder called `install` from your web server. The reason for this is that it contains the PHP code that configured your store. So it might be very easy for anybody who knows it is there to rerun the install process with erroneous information and mess up your store.

## Time for action – how to delete the install folder

This is probably the quickest and easiest way to do it:

1.  Press the *Windows* key and hit *E* once. This will bring up a new Explorer window.

2.  In the address bar, type `ftp://yourdomain.com` and hit *Enter/Return*.

3.  Enter your FTP username and password.

4.  Find the `install` folder. It is nice and prominent, near the top, under the `img` folder.

5.  Right-click on it and select **Delete**. That's it. Don't close the FTP window, and read on.

## *What just happened?*

Without the PrestaShop installation files, nobody can run the installation process again. So we just prevented anyone with a little bit of knowledge from reinstalling over our PrestaShop and causing us to have a bad day. Next we will take another precaution to protect our new shop.

# Renaming the admin folder

The `admin` folder holds all the web pages and PHP code that allows you to manage your shop. Almost any customization or configuration that you will make using your control panel, including the ability to log in, relies on this folder and the knowledge of its location. So you obviously you don't want any Tom, Dick, and Harry sitting on their PC at `www.yourdomain.com/admin` trying to guess your password. And anybody who knows anything about e-commerce software knows that the default folder name for such functions is often `admin`. So we will now name it something more secret and personal.

## Time for action – renaming the admin folder

You should already have an FTP window to perform these steps. If not, repeat steps 1 to 3 in the previous *Time for action* section and then come back here:

1. Find the `admin` folder.
2. Right-click on it and select **Rename**.
3. Rename it something that is easy to remember but difficult to guess.
   I suggest treating your `admin` folder name like a password. Perhaps, `admintrickypassword`. Make sure to leave the `admin` folder bit at the start. Then it would be safe from prying eyes and tampering fingers, but you and the PrestaShop system will know where it is.
4. Close your FTP window.

## *What just happened?*

You just made your store's control panel practically inaccessible to anybody except you.

# Your shop front explained

Now, at last, it is time to see your shop! Visit www.yourdomain.com. It should look like the following screenshot:

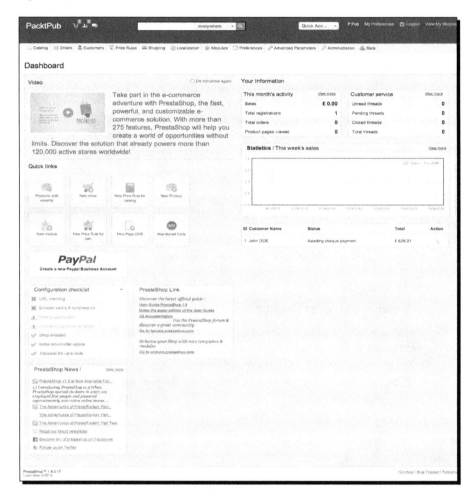

If you haven't already done this, then go and have a look at a PrestaShop that has some content. This will help you visualize approximately how your own store will take shape. You can do this at http://demo-store.prestashop.com/en/.

Now you can see the logo of your shop, a search bar, useful links such as **contact**, **sitemap**, or **bookmark**, select the **Currency** option, a **Log in** link, and the main menu in the top area of a website.

The following screenshot is the header. The header is the top area in a website:

On both sides of the web we have columns. On the left side, we have the main navigation.

On the right column, we have specials offers, latest products, and some information about your store.

In the middle of the website, we have the products. On the homepage there are featured products and one carousel, but when we surf along the categories, we see a list of products that belong to that category. When we click on a product, we have all the information about that product in this area.

The latest part of this area is called the footer. We have useful links and contact details in this area, as shown in the following screenshot:

# Your shop-back explained

Now log in to your store control panel. This is where 90 percent of this book will take place, because here, you will add all your products, check your sales, change the design of your store, and so on. This is what you will see:

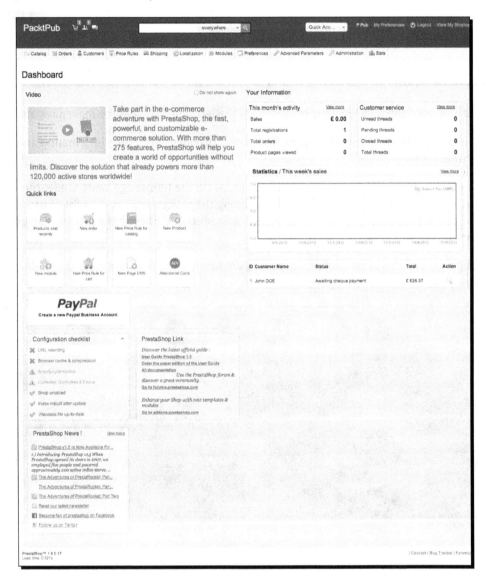

But if you see the following screenshot, you need to go back the *Post-install security* section.

# Time for action – logging in to your PrestaShop control panel

Here is how to get there:

1. In your web browser type `www.yourdomain.com/youradminfoldername`, where `youradminfoldername` is the same name that you chose for your `admin` folder previously.

2. Enter the e-mail address you registered with and the password you gave on the last configuration page, when you installed PrestaShop.

**3.** Hit enter and you're in.

**4.** Why don't you have a look at the PrestaShop live feed? This contains topical news and information about PrestaShop direct from the creators. If there is an update available for PrestaShop, you will hear about it here.

## What just happened?

You took your first look inside your store control panel. Now let's click some buttons.

# Control panel guided tour

Here I will quickly run through some of the general functions contained within each tab and drop-down box. I shall also mention the chapters in which we will cover them in more detail. Why not explore as we run through them? A full control panel reference is contained in *Appendix 1, Control Panel Quick Reference*. From left to right, we have:

- **Catalog**: On this tab we have everything we need to manage our product range and all related aspects. For example, as well as creating the products themselves (*Chapter 3, Merchandising for Success*), we can also give our customers manufacturer and supplier information to aid their buying decision (*Chapter 2, The Back Office*). We can assign advanced features to our catalog such as attributes, features, customizations, and attachments (*Chapter 3, Merchandising for Success*). We can also assign product tags to help customers and search engines easily find what they want (*Chapter 4, Getting More Customers*).

- **Orders**: Here we can manage every aspect of post-purchase communication such as notifying customers of dispatch or a problem, making invoices available, and printing packing slips. All of this will be covered in *Chapter 8, Ready to Sell*.

- **Customers**: The **Customers** tab allows us to view and edit our list of customers as well as creating groups of different types of customers. This, as we know, can be very useful (*Chapter 8, Ready to Sell*).

- **Price Rules**: This tab lets us customize your customers experience. Here we can create discounts for specific carriers, products, suppliers, categories, manufacturers, combinations, or offer free shipping. It also lets us create and manage gift vouchers that can be purchased (*Chapter 7, Checkouts and Shipping*) or given away as a promotion (*Chapter 8, Ready to Sell*).

- **Shipping**: Unfortunately, this tab can't actually deliver stuff for you. It does everything that is related to delivering your customers' orders. You can configure shipping types, costs, and durations in any combination to suit your business (*Chapter 7, Checkouts and Shipping*).

- **Localization**: Here we can set up our shop for different languages, zones, countries that we deliver, states, currencies, taxes and tax rules, and translations. We will also go into depth in *Chapter 7, Checkouts and Shipping*.

- **Modules**: Everything in PrestaShop is about module. If you put a shopping basket here, it's a module; if you put a menu there, it's a module. We will be in and out of the **Modules** tab all the time. We will also go into greater depth about modules in (*Chapter 2*, *The Back Office* and *Chapter 5*, *Tools, Newsletters, Extra Income, and Statistics*).

- **Preferences**: This is the second most varied tab in the whole of PrestaShop. There are many things you can do here. We will be popping in here from time to time and then covering everything we missed (*Chapter 5*, *Tools, Newsletters, Extra Income, and Statistics*).

- **Advanced Parameters**: Here we can check and set up different performances for our shop such as, cache, database backups, and logs (*Chapter 5*, *Tools, Newsletters, Extra Income, and Statistics* and *Chapter 6*, *Security and Disaster Recovery*).

- **Administration**: We manage our preferences, add, edit or delete employees, set up profiles, and permissions (*Chapter 6*, *Security and Disaster Recovery*).

- **Stats**: This topic is crucial. It is a very significant area where PrestaShop stands head and shoulders above its competitors. Capturing and using statistics (*Chapter 5*, *Tools, Newsletters, Extra Income, and Statistics*) will allow you to measure success and decide how to change and improve your shop (*Chapter 9*, *Go... To the Future*).

## Have a go hero – hunt the PrestaShop thimble

Here is a little challenge for you. Nothing very technical but a sort of PrestaShop "hunt the thimble". What if you wanted to temporarily disable your shop? Maybe you wanted to close it for maintenance. Perhaps you want to close it down during development when you're not actually viewing it. Can you find where to do it?

I promise you the solution is simple. But can you find out where is it hiding?

Solution: Click on the **Preferences** tab. Scroll down to **Maintenance** and select **No**. The Maintenance IP box even enables you to enter your unique Internet (IP) address so that only you can see the shop. This is a perfect, secure manner to develop your store. To get your IP address visit `http://www.whatsmyip.org/`. Enter it in the box on your **Preferences** tab and click on **Save**.

# Before we continue

It is not important to know where everything is and how it works at this stage. As I mentioned before, we will approach each topic in the likely order of setting up a new business and not in a left-to-right manner. I just thought it might be nice to have a look under the hood before we get stuck in! This will hopefully help you to master PrestaShop more logically and to achieve my 7-day challenge.

## Pop quiz – a few questions about Chapter 1

Q1. Many web hosts charge per database or have a limit before forcing you to upgrade your package. How would you create almost unlimited PrestaShop installations on the same domain name and same database without overwriting the original?

1. Upgrading your web host package

2. Enable multistore

3. Contract different web hosts

4. Contract different web hosts and domains

Q2. Once configured, which tab would you most likely use to know how many visitors have visited your website?

1. Module

2. Customers

3. Stats

4. Shipping

Q3. What do you think would be the fastest way (least clicks) to begin the process of creating a new product?

1. Click on **Catalog** and then click on **Product**

2. Click on **Catalog** and then click on **Categories**

3. Click on **Administration** and then click on **Menu**, then add Product to the menu

4. Click on **Preferences** and click on **Product**

# Summary

We learned a lot in this chapter about PrestaShop.

Specifically, we covered the following:

- Obtaining PrestaShop: Where to download it from and how to prepare the files, including how to transfer them via FTP to your website.

- MySQL databases: How PrestaShop uses the database, how to create a MySQL database, and how the different terms are used to refer to the database location.

- PrestaShop installer: How to complete each step of the installer and filling out the slightly trickier pages like the database configuration page, and how to get around an intermittent bug in the installer.

- The shop front: How to refer to different parts of the shop front.

- The shop back: A brief look at where the different functions and tasks can be performed.

We're now ready to fit your shop with a visually pleasing, unique, and sales-efficient design. This is the topic of the next chapter. So let's get stuck in!

# 2
# Back Office

*Your shop front, as it stands, is quite bland. But in about 20 pages time it will be bristling with modules, search boxes, navigation boxes, a smart header, and much more.*

In this chapter, we will:

- ◆ Set the shape of your store including the logo
- ◆ Build your home page
- ◆ Populate key website pages such as the contact us and conditions of use pages
- ◆ Configure manufacturer and supplier information
- ◆ Change and customize themes
- ◆ Add a few more touches to your shop's configuration

So let's get on with it...

# Dashboard

Dashboard is the landing page you get to when you log in to your back office. Here, you can take a quick look about your shop activity, customer services, statistics, configuration checklist, PrestaShop news and links, and quick links to different sections on the Web such as Products sold recently, new orders, or new products.

# Catalog

This section contains all the content that you want to sell to your customer. The **Products** subsection contains all the items that are in your store. The **Categories** subsection is the easiest way to keep a tidy store; to make it easier for our customers to find our products, we split our products into different categories. In the **Monitoring** section, we can track multiple issues of concern in your product inventory. **Attributes and Values** is the area where you can set up new attributes for your products, such as color, size, and so on. **Features** can relate to physical dimensions or other characteristics of the product. **Manufacturers** is the section where we add the companies that make a particular product. The **Suppliers** section contains the information that can help us get more products. **Image Mapping** is used to create a hotspot on an image. The **Tags** section is used for assigning short descriptions (tags) to the products. Sometimes, you may need to provide a file (such as a manual or software) as part of the product; this can be done in the **Attachments** section.

# Orders

This is the best part of an e-commerce shop; you will be able to see all the orders and everything that you sold. Also, this section will contain invoices, merchandise returns, delivery slips, credit slips, statuses, and order messages.

# Customers

Every customer or person that signed up will be shown in this section. Here you can check all the information about our clients. You may also split your customers in different groups, such as a VIP group, to offer different discounts or different products.

If any of your customers did not check out, you can see what they have in their shopping cart.

In this section, we will set up and detail the information on customer services and contacts. This is very important because if you take care of your clients, the clients speak well about your store, and that is the best publicity you can get for your shop.

# Price rules

This section could be one of our clients' favorites because this is where the vouchers and discounts for your clients are listed.

# Shipping and localization

If the products that you are selling are digital, then this section is not for you. In this section, we will set up the pricing, rules, and carriers to deliver your products.

Under localization, you can set up the different languages that you would like to offer on your website, all the countries that you want to sell your products to, taxes, and currencies.

# Modules

This is one of the most important sections on your site because this is where all the functionality and design is. For that, we will cover this section in detail.

## Arranging key modules

What is a module? A module is an independent widget that you can add to your e-commerce website. The best way of demonstrating this is to get on and do something.

First, I will list the key PrestaShop modules and their uses. I will then go through them step by step, enabling, configuring (whenever necessary), and positioning them. I will also suggest positions for the modules and give reasons for my suggestions.

It is important to remember that everyone's shop has varying objectives and it is perfectly reasonable, maybe even likely, that you would want to discard some of my suggestions. This is good, and if you feel like you know best after having read my suggestions and reasons, then you probably do know best. It's your shop, and that is the whole point of the flexibility of PrestaShop; every shop should be unique. There is no better option.

The following screenshot shows the **Modules** tab in your control panel:

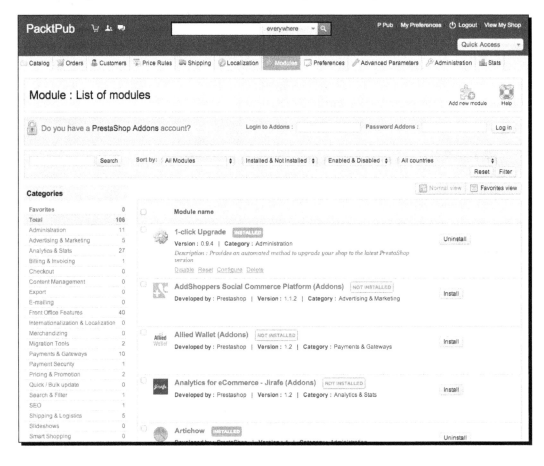

Take a look at the screenshot or click on the **Modules** tab in your PrestaShop control panel. On the left, we have a list of modules divided into categories; on the right, we have a list with the description and status of all the modules (installed or not installed) in our shop.

There are dozens of modules. We are just going to look at the most common or key examples. There are some key modules, such as payment modules (quite important for a shop), which we will skip now and deal with later in a specific section that deals with payment.

I will go into click-by-click detail in the *Time for action* section for the first module. I will go into the same level of detail whenever there is anything new or different, like when configuration options are required. But if the setup of a module is closely identical to a previous one, I will just point this out. You can then refer to a previous *Time for action* tutorial or set it up from memory. So let's get on with it.

# Cart block

Every self-respecting shop has a shopping cart. It is a part of the web page that summarizes the customer's current situation with regard to product choices. It will show an abbreviated list of all the items selected for possible purchase as well as the total amount of money due so far. I had said that I would make suggestions about the likely use of the different modules and I cannot think of any good reason why a shop would not display this particular module.

I would also suggest that it should be made highly prominent. Its very presence alerts visitors to the fact that you are a shop and not just an information website. Its effect is very similar to the physiological effect of a "real" shopping cart. If you haven't got one, you can't put anything in it!

Why not check a few of the major online retailers and see what they do with their shopping cart? Many, if not most, have it in the top or right-hand side column near the top. This is how I will show you how to position yours.

## Time for action – installing the shopping cart module

We are now going to create a shopping cart module:

1. Log in to your PrestaShop control panel and click on the **Modules** tab. You should see the same window that you saw in the previous screenshot.

2. When you scroll down the list of modules, you will see the **Cart block** module. Just to the right of the description, click on the **Install** button (it is installed by default).

3. Now scroll back to the **Cart block** module. Notice the word in green. Click on **Configure**.

4. Here you have the option to select an **Ajax cart**. AJAX is a suite of technologies that enables some really cool and smooth web effects. Sounds like a good idea? Thought so. The reason you have the option to switch AJAX off is that some older templates that we will look at later in this chapter do not get along with AJAX, so you will need to switch it off. For now at least, I suggest leaving it on. Click on **Save** when you're ready.

**5.** Go and have a look at your shop front. You should see a page similar to the one shown in the following screenshot. Why not click on the **Cart** and **Check out** buttons to see the effect? It is a good idea to understand the experience that your customers will get.

## What just happened?

Congratulations! The first of your many modules has been enabled.

# What goes on your home page?

First let's discuss what goes on the home page and then it's time for action to actually add your new content to the home page.

## Unique Selling Proposition (USP)

Every business should have a USP, that is, a reason in the form of a statement that compels customers to stick around and spend money at your shop. It is this USP that is a viable option to be displayed right at the top of your home page. So how do you decide on one?

You need to think about your business and your products. What makes you different and unique? What is your "thing" that people can buy, which is so brilliant that they would want to find out more? By "thing" I don't mean a product, I mean a benefit that a key product or range from your shop gives your customers (selling) and how you present it to them (the proposition).

Let's look at an example. How many shops sell teddy bears? There is probably a multitude of shops selling teddies. So a half-hearted "Welcome to my shop. We sell teddy bears, and we really look after our customers", although sincere, won't sell much fluff!

But if I think about what is unique and will benefit my customers, I will start making some progress. I sell teddies, and they are fluffy. So how fluffy are they? I happen to know that they are really fluffy. In fact, I can't remember ever hugging a teddy that was fluffier. But is fluffiness really a benefit to my customer? Who shops on my site? It is not three-year olds with Visa and American Express. No, they are mums and dads. So what benefit do mums and dads get from my products? They want a happy, secure, and safe little toddler who has a teddy bear that he/she really loves that didn't break the bank.

How about this: "At `Fluffyteddies.com`, all our bears are made from the perfect mix of natural and man-made fibers to guarantee that your special little one feels snuggled and loved by their new bear. And because we specialize only in bears and the like, we are never beaten on price."

A good USP is often made from a mixture of key facts, emotive reassurances, and a guarantee. Your USP could be much shorter: "The crumbliest, flakiest milk chocolate in the world" or "The softest, most huggable teddy bear at the picnic!"; it could also be much longer. What's important is that it is not just a greeting or a statement with facts, and it specifically reveals certain benefits to the purchaser.

## Time for action – how to add your content to your home page

PrestaShop has a really easy-to-use CMS. CMS is an acronym for Content Management System. It will allow you to create and label content and then enable links to it. We will see more of this when we create your "must have" pages, in a minute, and when we look at the CMS in more depth in *Chapter 4, Getting More Customers*. PrestaShop deals with home page content in a slightly different way. It uses another module called the **Home text editor**. Here goes:

1.  Click on the **Modules** tab and scroll down, find the **Image slider for your homepage** module, and click on **Install** (by default, it is installed).

2.  Now come back to it again and click on **Configure**. I have divided the page that you will see into two screenshots, one for the back office and the other for the home page.

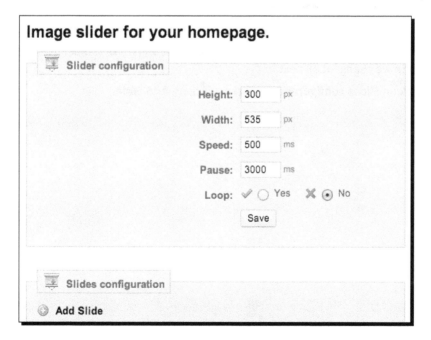

The following is a screenshot of your home page with a new slider:

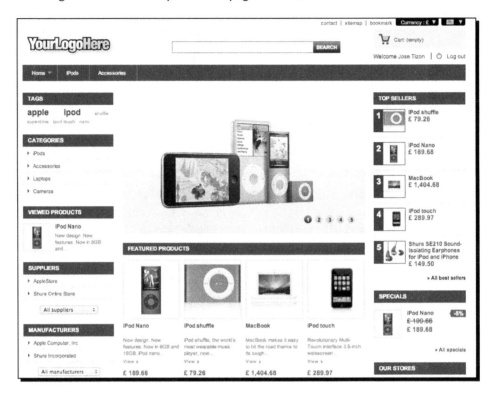

3.  Now visit your store's home page. This will show you what the default content in the **Image slider for your homepage** module is. This will make it much easier to follow when we change it all next.

4.  Click on **Slides configuration** and then click on **Add Slide**.

5.  Select the image that you want to display on your home page. Give it a title using the **Title** field, a link in the **URL** field, and a small brief in the **Legend** field. If you want to write something longer, then you can do this using the **Description** field. The last option here is, whether you want it to be active or not. This is very helpful when you are doing the campaign of a product and you do not want to show any more in the homepage. Remember, the fields file, title, URL and legend are required.

6.  Click on **Save** and you will have a nice image in the home page slider.

7.  Now we know how to add a new image to the slider, but to know everything about the **Image slider for your homepage** module, I am going to dig deeper into the slider configuration. This section is used to set the size of the images on our homepage. By default, the size is perfect for the default theme, but if you change your theme in the future (we will see how to do this in this chapter), you might need to change the size to fit the new design. Also, we can change the transition speed between images and the duration of time for which they will be paused. For that we have the fields, **Speed** and **Pause**; both numbers have to be in milliseconds. The last field in this area is **Loop**. If the loop option is on, all the images will show automatically, but if it is off, the customer will need to use slider navigation.

**8.** When you are happy with the configuration, click on **Save** and check whether your home page looks the way you want it to. Make corrections to this (if any) and then repeat this step until you are satisfied.

## What just happened?

You now have the most prominent page of your website. Take a look at your home page. It's coming together nicely, I think. Remember that you can and should update this page as and when it is relevant to do so.

With PrestaShop CMS, you can create your "must have" pages, such as the **About us**, **Terms and conditions of use**, or **Secure payment** pages.

## Secure payment

Secure payment is a guarantee for your clients that everything that they buy in your shop is safe to be paid for online. For that, it is essential for your shop to have secure payment modes and to display them on the website.

## Time for action – using the content management system

Having decided upon the text for all of your pages, it is time to actually create them.

**1.** Hover over the **Preferences** tab, and then click on **CMS**.

**2.** From the list of pages, click on the first one that you would like to edit. The **Edit** button is the one with the little pencil and paper picture in the middle of the three icons to the right.

**3.** Type in or copy and paste your content. Click on the **Save** button when done. One tip, if you decide to copy and paste from Microsoft Word or similar software, is to first paste the content in Notepad to clear Word formatting tags.

**4.** Repeat this procedure for each page. Notice that there is a little bin icon next to the edit icon. You can delete a page if you feel you do not need it. For example, many stores combine their terms and conditions with their legal notice.

**5.** Visit all your new pages to make sure that they are formatted as you want them to be.

## *What just happened?*

The "must have" pages are hardly the most exciting pages of your shop to be created. However, they are really important. And once they are done, you can usually leave them alone and get on to more exciting things! Next we will learn how to move modules around our store. Read on.

## Moving modules around

No technical jiggery-pokery required here. PrestaShop allows you to move modules around at will and decides whether there are any pages on which a module should not appear. Here is a lightning guide for doing just that.

## Time for action – moving modules

Make sure that you are logged into your PrestaShop control panel and then follow these steps:

*1.*  Hover over the **Modules** tab and then click on the **Positions** subtab.

*2.*  Click on the **Transplant a module** link.

3. Select the module that you would like to move in the first drop-down box at the top of the page, and then select the location you would like to move it to in the second one.

4. Now specify a list of any pages that you don't want the module to appear on (if any).

5. Click on **Save**.

6. Notice that the module appears twice, in the original position and the new one. If this is not the effect you desire, simply go back to your module positions page and click on the bin icon next to the one you don't want anymore.

7. Now you are back to the main **Positions** page. You can scroll down to the position you just moved a module to, and using the up and down arrow keys, raise or lower the position it appears in. You can also drag-and-drop the modules.

## What just happened?

Almost any module can go anywhere now. As usual, my recommendation is to do one change at a time because everything all at once might not work or look good together.

# Preferences

The **Preferences** tab has everything you need to customize your shop in different ways. You will find the following subsections under the **Preferences** tab:

◆ In the **General** subsection, we can set up security specifications such as the option to use the HTTPS protocol.

◆ The **Orders** preferences subsection can be used to set up a minimum purchase amount, enable guest checkout, and offer a gift-wrapping, among others.

◆ In the **Products** preferences subsection, you can choose to make certain products in your shop unavailable for sale. This is very useful when you need to do some restocking of your products or if you need to do maintenance. Also, here you can set up the number of products that you would like to show per page.

◆ Under the **Customers** preferences subsection, you can choose to show the last shopping cart to your customers or to regenerate password to have a security minimum time.

◆ The next subsection under the **Preferences** tab is **Themes**; we will dig deeper into this section later.

◆ In the **SEO & URLs** subsection, we can check for and set up search-friendly URLs and titles for our main pages.

The sizes of default images such as categories, products, scenes, and more can be defined by you. This is a really easy way to add more uniqueness to your shop. Also, you can create some great layouts and enhance your chosen template with just a few well-chosen dimensions.

## Time for action – changing the default image size

This is really easy to do. The trick to achieving something unique here is to experiment. Try some really big sizes and consider decreasing the number of products per page at the same time, especially if you have a small niche range or sell products with interesting or detailed images. Here is how:

**1.** Hover over the **Preferences** tab and then click on the **Images** subtab. Notice that you can change the size of just about any image. This is really flexible and useful. Try experimenting with different image types.

**2.** Click on the **Edit** button next to whichever image you are going to mess with and enter your new size. Be daring, you can always change it back. Click on **Save** when you are done.

**3.** Now scroll to the bottom of the page and click on **Regenerate thumbnails**. Go and have a look at your products. Some of the images might need to be edited in your CSS file, and for some you will see the change right away.

**4.** Now, we can also reduce the number of products per page (if necessary). Hover over the **Preferences** tab and then click on the **Products** subtab. Scroll down to the **Products per page** field and enter the number you want.

**5.** Go and have a look at the result. Repeat the steps and tweak it until you feel it is unique.

## What just happened?

You can now vary the image sizes in your store. If doing so improves the look of your shop, make sure you use images that look good in their new size.

Now we can go on to explore and discuss key aspects of PrestaShop.

# PrestaShop themes

Themes are what distinguish one PrestaShop-powered store from another. They define the color, graphics, and even the actual ambience of your store. For example, if you are running a shop selling guns, you will want a very different theme compared to the one selling teddy bears.

Themes are readily available for PrestaShop—many are free and many are not. What follows is a low down on where and how to find a theme for your shop. In my view, getting the right theme is only the beginning of creating the perfect look for your e-commerce establishment.

I strongly recommend hunting high and low for the theme that most closely suits your purposes and then installing it. All this is covered here and now. I also suggest, once you are up and running, that you embark on a process of further customization. This will truly separate your store from everyone else's and, along with all the other elements discussed in this book, leave you with an absolutely unique store.

The process of template customization is a bit more advanced than simply choosing and installing a ready-made template; we will explore the basics in a bit. It has to be said, however, that you might be completely happy without customizing. I have a real shop with the regular PrestaShop theme and it does just fine.

Let's get on with finding and installing a great template.

## Finding themes

First of all, you need to have plenty of great themes to choose from. Visit `http://addons.prestashop.com/en/3-templates-prestashop` to find a list of great resources.

## Choosing a great theme

Now here is how to pick a great one. If you visit one of the theme (template) resources listed on `http://addons.prestashop.com/en/3-templates-prestashop`, you can find some really sleek-looking templates. Very often, these will require an additional configuration change (as well as uploading files), which will all be covered in a bit.

Here is a quick word of warning when you're choosing a new template, especially when you're paying for it. Look at the substance of the layout and not just the images used for display in the template. Remember that, most probably, every single image that you see on the demo site will need replacing! Think about how cool it will look with your images instead. Is the template you are thinking of buying truly beautiful, or is it just the images that look good?

Installing a template takes only a couple of minutes, so try as many free ones as you like, and consider the advice I've given you carefully before getting your wallet out.

When you have found a truly beautiful theme and you are ready to try it out, read on. Also, remember that these days, a lot of people use their mobile and tablet to check a website, for that you will need to decide if you want your store to be deployable on more devices.

# Installing the themes

As I had mentioned before, installing a theme is nice and easy. It's choosing a theme that is the hard part.

## Time for action – installing a PrestaShop theme

Here's how to do it:

1. Download the template to your PC.

2. Hold down the Windows key and tap the *E* key twice. In one window, browse to your downloaded theme. In the other window, log in to your website via FTP.

3. On your website, browse to the themes folder.

4. Drag the new themes folder onto your website.

5. Now log in to your PrestaShop admin panel.

6. Click on the **Preferences** tab, and then on **Appearance**. Scroll to the bottom of the page, select your new template, and click on **Save**. How quick was that?

## What just happened?

You can now switch themes at will. After this quick pop quiz, we will look at making your theme completely unique.

## Pop quiz – themes and things

So how do you customize the theme? Maybe you like the general layout but want to change some elements?

Q1. How do you think you can change the elements of the actual template itself? (Here's a clue: it's not in your control panel.)

1. By going to the **Modules** section and then clicking on **Featured Products on the homepage**.

2. By editing the HTML template with CSS and JavaScript.

3. By going to the **Modules** section, then selecting **Modules & Themes Catalog**.

Q2. How do you change the background color?

1. By editing the CSS file of the theme.

2. By editing the JavaScript file of the theme.

Q3. How do you change the default images of your new template?

1.  By clicking on the **Themes** subtab under **Preferences** and then selecting your logo.

2.  By editing the CSS file of the theme.

3.  By downloading an external module for it.

# Customizing your template

Here, as the heading suggests, we will look at customizing our chosen template. Creating a template from scratch is too in-depth for the space we have here and involves a skill I am not qualified to teach. The skill I am referring to is design. "Click here", "Click there" type of instructions don't help when trying to design something. If you really want to start from scratch, I would recommend you to get two kinds of books: the first on CSS, and another on design and layout principles.

The beauty of customizing an existing template is that all the tricky coding has been done for us; all we need to do is identify key elements of somebody else's work and make amendments to it. We can then choose a template whose overall shape and style we like, and use it as a starting point; we can change it in subtle or not so subtle ways to better suit our business and to make sure that our website is unique.

Now we will look at some "quick wins" for simple customization, then the PrestaShop template, and then discuss changing the CSS code that defines a template.

To do all this, I will be working with the default PrestaShop template, but everything I talk about should be just as relevant, regardless of your chosen template. So let's get on with it.

## Important preliminary point

Throughout this part of the chapter, I will be making suggestions for you to change this and that, delete this, add that. It is very possible that it could all go horribly wrong. Therefore, you could be left with a template and a shop that doesn't work. Make sure you have a current backup of every file you alter and only make one change at a time, check the effect, and then move on. You have been warned!

# Time for action – creating a new template

It's really easy to create a new template. The trick to achieving something unique here is to experiment. Try some really big sizes and perhaps consider decreasing the number of products per page at the same time, especially if you have a small niche range or sell products with interesting or detailed images. Here's how:

1.  Open an FTP window on your web host.

2.  Click on the `themes` directory in the main `prestashop` folder. Drag a copy of the folder you want to copy onto your desktop. If you're working with the default theme, the folder is called `prestashop`.

3.  Now right-click on the folder on your desktop and select **Rename**. Rename the folder to whatever you want your new theme to be called (no spaces and all lower case is the best convention).

4.  Drag the new folder onto your web server. You now have a new theme. You can use FileZilla to connect to your host; it is an open source software like PrestaShop.

5.  In your PrestaShop control panel, click on the **Preferences** tab and then click on **Themes**.

6.  Scroll to the bottom of the section and change to your new theme. Visit your shop, it will look no different. But now we can start to play with things.

## What just happened?

We now have a canvas, so to speak, which we can start to do wonderful things with. So let's do it.

## Editing your CSS file

The file that we are going to play with is called `global.css`. It is in the CSS folder inside our main template folder. A good way of working with it is to open it using a program like Notepad++ or something similar. Notepad++ is good because it does not add any extra formatting to a document, which is important. You can get a free copy of Notepad++ from `www.notepad-plus-plus.org`.

We can make one change at a time, upload it to the live folder on the web server, and then go view the changes. Like it? Great! Don't like it? Change it back and rethink the changes you would like to see.

First, I will point out a few parts of the CSS file that you can make interesting changes to, then I will guide you through a quick tutorial to show you how to implement the changes. I will discuss several potential changes all at once, but remember to do it one at a time and to make a backup at regular intervals. Why not open up `global.css` now and have a look.

If you don't understand CSS, it will look very confusing. A complete explanation, as you might guess, is way beyond the scope of this book. The good news is that, generally speaking, the code is quite easy to interpret and it uses English words to help identify the purpose of each part of the code. So we can scan through it and pick out the parts we'd like to change. The screenshot shows a couple of examples to get you started:

```css
1   /* ################################################################################
2       PRESTASHOP CSS
3   ################################################################################ */
4
5   @import url("grid_prestashop.css");
6
7   /* *********************************************************************
8           reset
9   ********************************************************************* */
10  html{color:#000;background:#FFF;}
11  body,div,dl,dt,dd,ul,ol,li,h1,h2,h3,h4,h5,h6,pre,code,form,fieldset,legend,input,button,textarea,p,blockquote,th,td{margin:0;padding:0}
12  table{border-collapse:collapse;border-spacing:0}
13  fieldset,img{border:0}
14  address,caption,cite,code,dfn,em,th,var,optgroup{font-style:inherit;font-weight:inherit}
15  del,ins{text-decoration:none}
16  caption,th{text-align:left}
17  h1,h2,h3,h4,h5,h6{font-size:100%}
18  q:before,q:after{content:''}
19  abbr,acronym{border:0;font-variant:normal}
20  sup{vertical-align:baseline}
21  sub{vertical-align:baseline}
22  legend{color:#000}
23  input,button,textarea,select,optgroup,option{font-family:inherit;font-size:inherit;font-style:inherit;font-weight:inherit}
24  input,button,textarea,select{font-size:100%}
25  a {cursor:pointer}
26
27  .clearfix:before,
28  .clearfix:after {
29      content: ".";
30      display: block;
31      height: 0;
32      overflow: hidden
33  }
34  .clearfix:after {clear: both}
35  .clearfix {zoom: 1}
36
37
38  /* *********************************************************************
39          struture
40  ********************************************************************* */
41  #page {}
42      #header {z-index:10}
43      #columns {z-index:1}
44          #left_column {}
45          #center_column {}
46          #right_column {}
47      #footer {}
48
49
50  /* *********************************************************************
51          generic style
52  ********************************************************************* */
53  body{
54      font:normal 11px/14px Arial, Verdana, sans-serif;
55      color:#222;
56      background:#fff
```

# Background color

On line number 56 in the previous screenshot, you can change the entire background color in a stroke. Just change the word `white` to any CSS-recognized color. A few examples are `aqua`, `black`, `blue`, `fuchsia`, `gray`, `green`, `lime`, `maroon`, and `navy`. A full list can be found at `www.w3schools.com/css/css_colors.asp`.

# Font size

You can easily guess that this element determines the size of the font. Scroll through your `global.css` file. You can see dozens of references to font size; they will all change the size of the font at different places.

```
50    /* ***************************************************
51          generic style
52    ***************************************************
53    body{
54        font:normal 11px/14px Arial, Verdana, sans-serif;
55        color:#222;
56        background:#fff
57    }
```

Scroll down to line number 54 (shown in the preceding screenshot) and change the value of `11px/14px` to `14px/14px`. From the context, can you guess where the font size will be changed? Try it out and then check the total amount for your shopping cart. Press *F5* to refresh your browser.

# Themes summary

You have probably guessed that the key to making your chosen template unique and stylish at the same time is a combination of all the things we have discussed, along with a bit of extra research into the CSS elements. As usual, don't put off further development or expansion of your business until you have achieved the perfect template because that day might never come.

As I mentioned at the beginning of this section, CSS and template design is a huge topic. If it is a topic that you want to find out about in detail, further reading is essential. If you just want a smart, unique template in a hurry, move on to the next phase of building your shop. Hopefully I have provided enough information here.

The other key factor in building a great template has got to be planning. I didn't mention this until the end because it definitely helps to experiment a bit. Until you know what is possible, it is hard to imagine what you would like to achieve. When you look at a template, try and envision how you could change it to make it yours.

For more information about templates, visit the PrestaShop forum. There is a whole section devoted to the subject at `www.prestashop.com/forums`.

## Time for action – uploading your company/store logo

So you now have your logo graphic. Here is how to add it to your shop:

1. Click on the **Preferences** tab.

2. Click on **Themes**. The next screenshot shows what you will see:

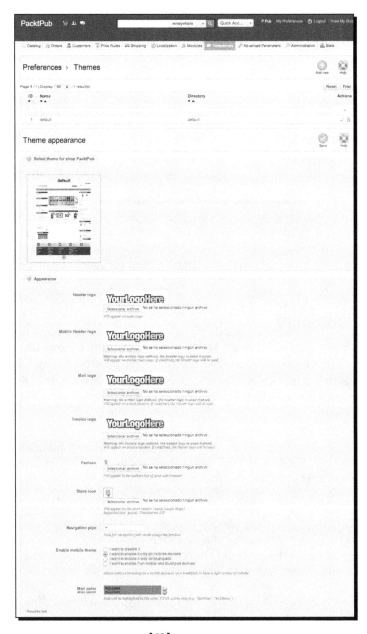

3. Click on the **Choose File** button underneath the **YourLogoHere** logo and browse to your new logo.

4. While on this screen, you can also upload a new favicon. This is a tiny graphic that is displayed in your visitors' web browser. Just make a 16 x 16 pixels image in GIMP and save it with the `.ico` extension.

5. When you're done, save the changes by clicking on **Save**.

## What just happened?

You now have a neat, well-optimized logo. It is starting to look like your very own PrestaShop.

# Advanced parameters and administration

In this section, we can check how our server is working and set up new backups for our database, among others.

The **Configuration Information** subsection is where we get to see all the configuration information that our server is giving us and whether it is in accordance with our PrestaShop store, and also whether there are some missing files.

The **Performance** tab is important to set up a cache for our site. Caching is a technique to save documents (HTML pages, images, and so on) temporarily to reduce bandwidth and connections to our database, we then get a faster service.

The **E-mail** tab lists the e-mail to which customers send messages from the orders page.

The **DB Backup** tab can be used to do a backup of our database. It is very important to keep in mind that we need to do backups very often because if something goes wrong with our hosting, we could lose all our information. This in turn would mean that we would not be able to sell any of our products, especially in cases where we have deadlines. To avoid such a situation, please do a backup of your database and files at regular intervals of time.

Logs are bits of information about what's happening in our shop. Here we can check whether there are any issues in our system. There are four levels to categorize this information. The first level, level 1, is just informative; levels 2 and 3 are warnings and errors in the system; if you have a level 4, then your shop is crashing and you need to fix it as soon as possible to keep it up and running.

# Time for action – making a customer account

Now it is time to create an account for yourself in your own shop. This will be useful now, and later as well. It is especially useful because the **My Account** module is only visible to customers who have logged in. Follow these steps to create your own account:

*1.* Click on **Your Account** at the top-right corner of your store's front end. In the **CREATE YOUR ACCOUNT** box, enter your e-mail ID and click on the **Create your account** button.

*2.* The form is self-explanatory. Fill it out and click on the green **Register** button at the bottom of the screen. You are now on the **My Account** page, as shown in the following screenshot:

## What just happened?

Now you have a customer account, which as we saw is useful for testing. You have also checked out the **My Account** block, which should help you decide whether you want one in your PrestaShop store.

Just in case you are not sure whether you want this module, consider your customers and your future store. Will your store be a place that is regularly visited by repeat purchase customers? For example, my website Bikes4U.com sells bikes and bicycle parts. I don't think the average Bikes4U customer would need a permanent link to their orders, credit slips, delivery addresses, and so on. The home page could be used to highlight special offers or new products like new arrivals or bestsellers.

However, FluffyTeddies.com also sells a huge range of build-it-yourself dolls, houses, and furniture. I expect enthusiasts to be constantly adding to their collections, checking on the progress of their orders, and buying vouchers for friends and family. They would also probably be interested in ordering gift items to be sent to alternate shipping addresses. A **My Account** module will definitely be useful in the teddy shop.

# Permanent links block

This block can be found in roughly the same place as all the modules so far. Install it and visit your shop front. Notice that you now have three key links added to the top of your store. They are: **contact**, **sitemap**, and **bookmark**. Why not try them all now? See what they do.

Your **sitemap** page has been very cleverly created for you. As you add products and other pages, PrestaShop updates your site map. The **contact** page consists of a contact form for your customers or soon-to-be customers to be able to quickly and easily contact you. Notice the **Subject Heading** drop-down box? We will talk more about that later in the chapter. And the **bookmark** button enables visitors to bookmark your site just a little bit quicker than by clicking on the button in their web browser.

# Stats

Here we can see how our customers use our website, what items are bestsellers, and the time and date at which you have a peak hour.

All of this information is very important and comes in handy when a particular area is not working fine for the customer or when you need to work on a new campaign to focus on an area.

# Creating the "must have" pages

What follows here, is a discussion of the pages you would probably expect to find on any e-commerce website. I will go through each in turn, discuss their purpose, and make some suggestions about creating your own version of the page.

## Delivery

This should contain everything a customer, future or current, needs to know about the delivery times, return, and refund policies. Depending upon the complexity of your offering, this whole page might amount to a couple of paragraphs or more.

## Legal notice

This page attempts to disclaim any unreasonable liabilities that you might encounter. Even if your content and products are not controversial, you might want to get proper legal advice for them.

Obviously, however, if you sell something that could leave you open to legal action, then you should definitely get proper legal advice and probably insurance as well.

This is one of the few areas where it might be worth getting your wallet out!

## Terms and conditions

They are many rules and regulations that you might have to draft for your customers and visitors. Often, this can be incorporated into the legal notice. The default template mentioned before has sample terms and conditions for you to amend, leave, or get legal advice on as you see fit.

## About us

This is the place to put the non-sales, non-product-specific stuff that so many new e-commerce sites make the mistake of putting on their home page. You can write this much better than I can.

What are your values? How long have you been in the business? Have you got an interesting startup story? How big is your business?

Your aim is to not sell anything other than YOU. Build trust and familiarity so that when your visitors find a product they want, they feel all warm and friendly towards you. Only then will they get their wallets out.

# Contacting your store

What if someone needs to contact you? Perhaps they need to ask a question, complain, or just say hello.

# Contacts

You need to have relevant contacts for the different types of messages that people could send. Don't panic, you don't need to employ staff. All you need to do is tell PrestaShop that certain types of message go to different e-mail addresses. This makes you look more professional and ensures that your customers don't feel like their message is not going into an empty black hole to be ignored.

## Time for action – creating departments to contact

We are going to divide your shop into departments to give it a more professional feel and to create confidence in the customers that send you messages. Remember that when we create these contacts and assign e-mail addresses, you will need to have previously created them through your hosting account.

1. Hover over the **Preferences** tab and then click on **Store Contacts**.

2. Click on **Add new** and enter the details of the new department/contact. Make sure you enter something informative in the **Note** box, because this is displayed to the customer. Then save the information.

3. Repeat the preceding steps for each department/e-mail address combination you require.

4. Visit your **contact** page and send test messages to each department to make sure everything is working as expected.

## *What just happened?*

You just made your shop seem much more professional.

# Multistore feature

The multistore feature is a new functionality in PrestaShop 1.5. With this functionality, you can easily manage several stores at once with only one back office, which means that it will make your life easier.

Every store is independent, but you could share categories, products pages, and so on. This functionality is very useful if you're working with different markets.

# Downloadable products

A downloadable product is an item that we do not need to ship. These kinds of items are usually songs in the `.mp3` format, books in the `.pdf` format, or software.

When we are selling an item like this, and we choose to add a new product, we have to choose the type of item on the main page; in this case, it will be **Virtual Product**. After this is done, PrestaShop will ask whether this product has an associated file; we need to click on **Yes** and we can then upload the file to sell.

# Are you an existing user of osCommerce? Let's import it to PrestaShop

If you have been working with osCommerce, welcome to PrestaShop. Importing all your information is very easy. The first thing that you have to do it is to go to **Modules**, then scroll down to **Importer osCommerce** on the modules list and click on the **Install** button. Once you have this module installed, you will need to follow the same process as the one detailed before, but with the module **Shop Importer**.

When you have both modules installed and active, click on **Configure link** under **Shop Importer**. You will then see a drop-down menu. Select **Importer osCommerce** and click on **Choose**. Fill in all the fields and click on **Import** to start the process.

# Summary

We achieved quite a lot in this chapter. Specifically, we covered:

- Setting up the key PrestaShop modules: With a few clicks, we can add or remove some very significant features to or from our store.

- Creating content for our home page: The home page is vital and should be updated frequently. It is controlled by a module.

- Creating our "must have" pages: PrestaShop has an easy-to-use Content Management System (CMS). This makes the creation and management of unique pages really fast and easy. There's more on the CMS in *Chapter 4, Getting More Customers*.

- Switching themes: It is not difficult to use a ready-made theme to customize our PrestaShop store.

- Learning how to make basic but significant customizations to our chosen theme.

Now that you have got a shop with essential pages, features, and content, it is time to give our customers some products to buy. That is the subject of the next chapter.

# Merchandising for Success

**3**

*Every successful e-commerce business needs to be customer-centric because without customers, our business would fail miserably. So always try to make your store easy, enjoyable and as fun as possible.*

In this chapter, we shall cover everything to display our products, and we will:

◆ Discuss and implement an efficient UX

◆ Discuss and implement an efficient category structure

◆ Add high quality product descriptions that sell

◆ Take a look at all the different ways you can use PrestaShop to highlight products

◆ Look at product features, attributes, accessories, and customization

So let's get on with it...

## Shop categories

Creating product categories, like most things in PrestaShop, is easy and we will cover that soon. First we need to plan the ideal category structure, and this demands a little thought.

# Planning your category structure

You should think really hard about the following questions: What is your business key – general scope or specific? Remember, if the usability is complex for you, it will be difficult to get future customers. So what will make the navigation simple and intuitive for your customers? What structure will support any plan you might have for expanding the range in the future? What do your competitors use? What could you do to make your structure better for your customers than anybody else's? When you have worked it out, we will create the category structure and then we will create the content (images and descriptions) for your category pages.

First you need to consider what categories you want for your product range. Here are some examples:

If your business is geared to the general scope, then it could be something like:

- Books
- Electronics
- Home and garden
- Fashion, jewelry, and beauty

However, if your business is a closed market, for example electronics, then it could be something like:

- Cameras and photography
- Mobile and home phones
- Sound and vision
- Video games and consoles

You get the idea.

My examples don't have categories, subcategories, or anything deeper just for the sake of it. There are no prizes for compartmentalizing. If you think a fairly flat structure is what your customer wants, then that is what you should do.

If you are thinking, "Hang on, I don't have any categories let alone any subcategories," don't panic. If your research and common sense says you should only have a few categories without any subcategories, then stick to it. Simplicity is the most important thing. Pleasing your customer and making your shop intuitive for your customer will make you more money than obscure compartmentalizing of your products.

## Creating your categories

Have your plan close at hand. Ideally, have it written down or, if it is very simple, have it clearly in your head. Enough of the theory, it is now time for action.

## Time for action – how to create product categories

Make sure that you are logged into your PrestaShop back office. We will do this in two steps. First we will create your structure as per your plan, then in the next *Time for action* section, we will implement the category descriptions. Let's get on with the structure of your categories:

1. Click on **Catalog** and you will see the categories. Click on one.

2. Now click on the green + symbol to add a new subcategory. PrestaShop defines even your top-level categories as subcategories because the home category is considered to be the the top-level category.

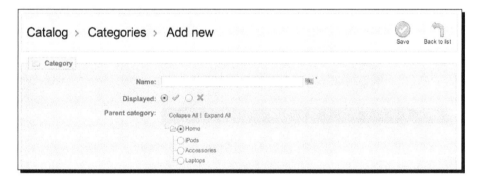

**3.** Just type in the title of your first main category. Don't worry about the other options. The descriptions are covered in a minute and the rest is to do with the search engines, which is covered in *Chapter 4, Getting More Customers*. Click on **Save** when you're done.

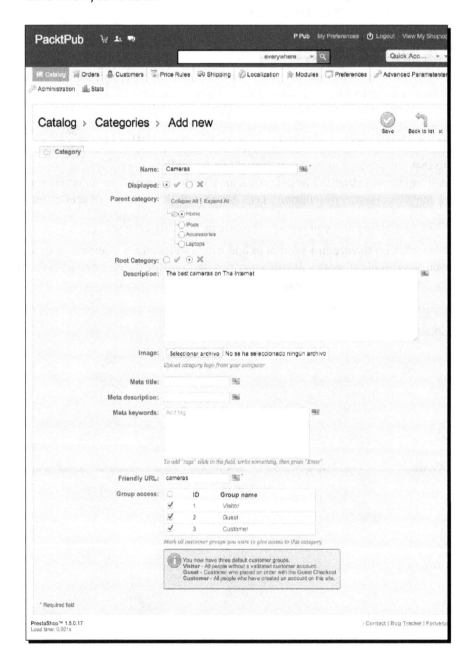

**4.** You have created your first category.

**5.** Now that you are back to the home category, you can click on the green button again to create your next main category. To do so, save as before and remember to check the **Home** radio button, when you are ready, to create your next main category.

**6.** Repeat until all top-level categories are created. Have a quick look at your shop front to make sure you like what you see. Here is a screenshot from the PrestaShop demo store:

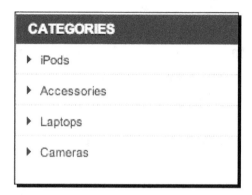

**7.** Now for the subcategories. We will create one level at a time as earlier. So we will create all the subcategories before creating any categories within subcategories. In your home category, you will have a list of your main categories. Click on the first one in the list that requires a subcategory.

**8.** Now click on the create subcategory + icon. Type the name of your subcategory, leaving the other options, and click on **Save**.

**9.** Go back to the main category if you want to create another subcategory.

**10.** Play around with clicking in and out of categories and subcategories until you get used to how PrestaShop works. It isn't complicated, but it is easy to get lost and start creating stuff in the wrong place. If this happened to you, just click on the bin icon to delete your mistake. Then pay close attention to the category or subcategory you are in and carry on. You can edit the **category order** from the main catalog page by selecting the box of the category you want to move and then clicking an up or down arrow.

**11.** Finish creating your full category structure. Play with the category and subcategory links on your shop front to see how they work and then move on.

## What just happened?

Superb! Your category structure is done and you should be fairly familiar with navigating around your categories in your control panel.

Now we can add the category and subcategory descriptions. I left it empty until now because as you might have noticed, the category creation palaver can be a bit fiddly and it makes sense to keep it as straightforward as possible. Here are some tips for writing good category descriptions followed by a quick *Time for action* section for entering descriptions into the category itself.

## Creating content for your categories and subcategories

I see so many shops online with really dull category descriptions. Category descriptions should obviously describe but they should also sell! Here are a few tips for writing some enticing descriptions:

- Keep them short—two paragraphs at the most. People do not visit your website to read.

- The detail should be in the products themselves. Similar to a USP, category descriptions should be a combination of fact and emotive description that focuses on the benefit to the customer.

- Try and be as specific as you can about each category and subcategory so that each description is accurate and relevant in its own right. For example, don't let the category steal all the glory from a subcategory.

- It is very important for SEO.

## Time for action – adding category descriptions

Be ready with the text for all your categories or you can, of course, type them as you go:

1. Go to **Catalog** and then on the first categories' **Edit** button.

2. Enter your category description and click on **Save**.

3. Click on the subcategories of your first category. Then enter and save a description for each (if any).

4. Navigate to the second main category and enter a description. Repeat the same for each of the subcategories in turn.

5. Reiterate the preceding steps for each category.

## What just happened?

You now have a fully functioning category structure.

Now we can go on to look at adding some of your products.

# Adding products

Click on the **Catalog** tab and then click on **product**. It is pretty similar to category.

In the *Time for action* section, I will cover what to enter in each box as a separate item. However, I will skip over a few items like meta tags because they are best dealt with on a site-wide basis separately.

The other important option is the product description. This deserves special treatment because it needs to be effective at selling your product.

With the categories, I specifically showed you how to create the structure before filling in the descriptions because I know others who have got into a muddle in the past. It is less likely, but still possible, to get into a bit of a muddle with the products as well. This is especially true if you have lots of them.

Perhaps you should be the judge of whether to fill in your catalog before adding descriptions or add descriptions as you go. So here is a handy guide to create great product descriptions. It will help you to decide whether you should fill product descriptions at the same time as the rest of the details, or whether you should just enter the product title and revisit them later to fill in the rest of the details.

# Product descriptions that sell

Don't fall into the trap of simply describing your products. It might be true that a potential customer does need to know the dry facts like sizes and other uninspiring information, but don't put this information in the brief description or description boxes. PrestaShop provides a place for bare facts—the **Features** tab (there will be more on this soon).

The brief description and description boxes that will be described in more detail soon are there to sell to your customers—to increase their interest to a level that makes them "want" the product. It actually suggests they pop it in their cart and buy it.

The way you do this is with a very simple and age-old formula that actually works. And, of course, having whetted your appetite, it would be rude not to tell you about it. So here it goes.

## Actually selling the product

Don't just tell your customers about your product, sell them the product. Explain to them why they should buy it! Use the FAB technique—feature, advantage, benefit:

◆ Tell the customer about a feature:

❑ This teddy bear is made from a new fiber and wool mix

❑ This laptop has the brand new i7 processor made by Intel

❑ This guide was written by somebody who has survived cancer

◆ And the advantage that feature gives them:

❑ So it is really, really soft and fluffy!

❑ i7 is the very first processor series with a DDR3 integrated memory controller!

❑ So all the information and advice is real and practical

◆ Then emphasize the real emotive benefit this gives them:

❑ Which means your little boy or girl is going to feel safe, loved, and secure with this wonderful bear

❑ Meaning that this laptop gives your applications, up to a 30 percent performance boost over every other processor series ever made

❑ Giving you or your loved one the very best chance of beating with cancer and having more precious time they have with the people they love

Don't just stop at one feature. Highlight the most important features. By most important features, of course I mean the features that lead to the best most emotive and personal benefits. Not too many though. If your product has loads of benefits, then try and pick just the best ones.

Three is perfect. Three really is a magic number. All the best things come in threes and scientific research actually proves that thoughts or ideas presented in threes influence human emotion the most. If you must have more than three features, summarize them in a quick bulleted list. Three is good:

◆ Soft, strong, and very long

◆ Peace, love, and understanding

◆ Relieves pain, and clears your nose without drowsiness

## Ask for the sale

When you have used the FAB technique, ask the customer to part with their money! Say something like, "Select the most suitable option for you and click on **Add to cart**" or "Remember that abc is the only xyz with benefit 1, benefit 2, and benefit 3. Order yours now!"

## Create some images with GIMP

If you have a favorite photo editor then great. If you haven't, then I suggest you use GIMP. It's cool, easy, and free: `www.gimp.org`.

## Time for action – how to add a product to PrestaShop

Let's add some products:

*1.* Click on catalog and then click on product.

**2.** Click on the **Add a new product** link. You will see the following screenshots. Okay, I admit it. It does look a little bit daunting. But actually it is not that difficult. Much of it is optional, and even more we will revisit after further discussion. So don't despair. There is a table of explanations for you after the screenshots.

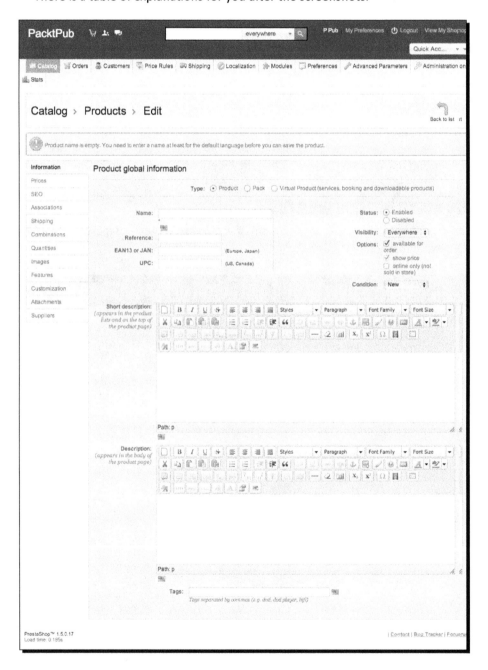

| Field | Explanation |
| --- | --- |
| **Name** | The short name/description of your product. There is a brief description and a full description box later, but perhaps a bit more than a short name should go here. |
| | For example, 50 cm golden teddy bear—extra fluffy version. |
| **Status** | Choose **Enabled** or **Disabled**. If your product is for sale as soon as you're open, click **Enabled**. If your product is discontinued or needs to be removed from sale for any reason, click **Disabled**. |
| **Reference** | An optional unique reference for your product. |
| | For example, 50cmFT – xfluff. |
| **EAN13** | The European Article Number or barcode. If your product has one (and almost everything does), use it because some people use this for searching or identifying a product. |
| **Jan** | The Japanese Article Number or barcode. If your product has one (and almost everything does), use it because some people use this for searching or identifying a product. |
| **UPC** | The USA and Canadian Article Number or barcode. If your product has one (and almost everything does), use it because some people use this for searching or identifying a product. |
| **Visibility** | If you want to show the item on the catalog, only on the search or everywhere. |
| **Type** | You can chose if there is a physical product, pack, or a downloadable product. |
| **Options** | To make the product available/unavailable to order. To show or hide the price. To enable/disable the online message. |
| **Condition** | If the item is brand new, second hand, or refurbished. |
| **Short description** | Here you need to add a brief description about the item. This text will be shown on the catalog. |
| **Description** | When a customer clicks on the item, he will read this text. |
| **Tags** | More on this in *Chapter 4, Getting More Customers*. Leave blank for now. |

**3.** Fill in your product page as described previously.

**4.** Click on the **Images** tab at the top of the product page.

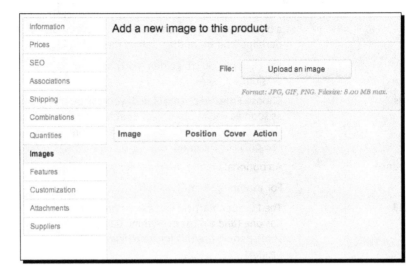

**5.** Browse to the image you created earlier and upload it. Note that PrestaShop will compress the image for you. It is worth having a look at the final image and maybe varying the amount (if any) that you apply when creating your product images.

**6.** Click on **Save** and then go and admire your product in your store front.

**7.** Repeat until all your products are done, but don't forget to check how things look from the customer's point of view. Visit the category and product pages to check whether things are like the way you had expected them to be. If you have a huge range that is going to take you a long time, then consider just entering your key products. Proceed with this book to get the money coming in and add the rest of your range in a bit over the course of time.

## What just happened?

Now you have something to actually sell, let's go and showcase some of your products. Here is how to make some of your products stand out from the crowd.

# Highlighting products

Next is a list of the different ways to promote elements of your range. There is also an explanation of each option and how to do it, as well.

# New products

So you have just found some great new products. How do you let your visitors know about it? You could put an announcement on your front page. But what if a potential customer doesn't visit your front page or perhaps misses the announcement?

Welcome to the new products module.

## Time for action – how to highlight your newest products

The following are the quick steps to enable and configure the highlighting of any new products you add. Once this is set up, it will happen automatically, now and in the future.

1. Click on the **Modules** tab and scroll down to the **New products block** module.
2. Click on **Install**.
3. Scroll back down to the module you just installed and click on **Configure**.
4. Choose a number of products to be showcased and click on **Save**.
5. Don't forget to have a look at your shop front to see how it works. Click around a few different pages and see how the highlighted product alternates.

### *What just happened?*

Now you are done with new products and they will never go unnoticed.

## Specials

Special refers to the price. This is the traditional special offer that customers know and love.

## Time for action – creating a special offer

The following steps help us create special offers and make sure they will never go unnoticed:

1. Click on the **Catalog** tab and navigate to the category or subcategory that contains the product you want to make available as a special offer.
2. Click on the **Products** to go to its details page.

**3.** Click on **Prices** and go to the **Specific prices** section.

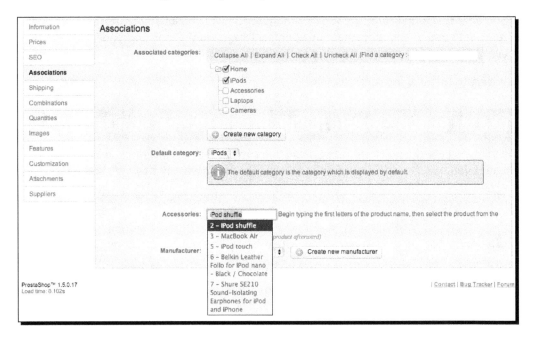

**4.** Click on **Add a new specific price**.

**5.** You can enter an actual monetary amount in the first box or a percentage in the second box. Monetary amounts work well for individual discounts and percentages work well as part of a wider sale. But this is not a hard-and-fast rule. So choose what you think your customers might prefer. Click on **Save**.

**6.** Now go and have a look at the category that the product is in and click on the product as well. You'll notice the smart enticing manner that PrestaShop uses to highlight the offer. You can have as many or as few special offers as you like.

**7.** But what if you wanted to really push a product offer or a wider sale? Yes, you guessed it, there's a module.

**8.** Click on the **Modules** tab and scroll down to **Specials block** and click on **Install**. Getting the hang of this? Thought so.

**9.** Go and have a look at the effect on your store.

## What just happened?

Your first sale is underway.

## Recently viewed

What's this then? When customers browse products, they forget what they have seen or how to find it again. By prominently displaying a module with their most recent viewings, they can comfortably click back and forth comparing until they have made a buying decision. Now you don't need me to tell you how to set this up. Go to the module, switch it on, and you're done.

## Best sellers

This is just what it says. Not necessarily an offer or anything else is special about it. But if it sells, well there must be something worth talking about it. Install the best sellers module in the usual place to highlight these items.

## Accessories

I love accessories. It's all about add-on sales. Ever been to a shop to buy a single item and come out with several? Electrical retailers are brilliant at this. Go in for a PC and come out with a printer, scanner, camera, ink, paper, and the list goes on. Is it because their customers are stupid? Of course they are not! It is because they offer compelling or essential accessories that are relevant to the sale. By creating accessories, you will get a new tab at the bottom of each relevant product page along with PrestaShop making suggestions at key points of the sale.

All we have to do is tell PrestaShop what is an accessory to our various products and PrestaShop will do the rest.

# Time for action – creating an accessory

Accessories are products. So any product can be an accessory of any other product. All you have to do is decide what is relevant to what. Just think about appropriate accessories for your products and read on. The quick guide for creating accessories are as follows:

1. Click on the **Catalog** tab, then click on product. Find the product you think should have some accessories.

2. Click on it to edit it by navigating to **Associations** on the page and find the **Accessories** section, as shown in the following screenshot:

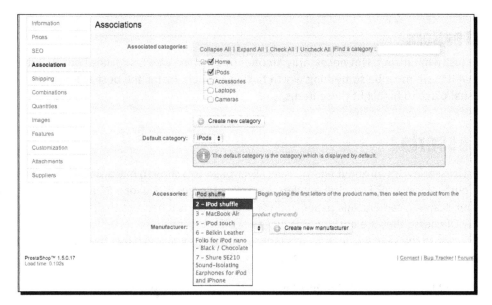

3. Find the product that you wish to be an accessory by typing the first letters of the product name and selecting it.

4. Save your amended product. You can add as many accessories to each product as you like.

5. Go and have a look at your product on your shop front and notice the **Accessories** tab.

## *What just happened?*

You just learned how to accessorize. It's silly not to accessorize, not because it costs you nothing, but because a few clicks could significantly increase your turnover.

Now we can go on to explore more product ideas.

# Features

This is very useful. Suppose you have a range of products and they all have features in common. Take, for instance, teddy bears. They are all made of something. But what if you want to have different groups for material or for size, and you need a simple solution for making that information available without polluting the product description? An example would be useful.

I have a range of teddy bears and they are made from super-soft cotton, micro-fiber, or wool knit. So I create a feature and call it "Material". I can then create a range of "Values" for "Material" such as super-soft cotton, micro-fiber, and wool knit. And I can assign values to any products that I choose.

You can create as many features and associated values as you need. You might want a country of origin feature, with assigned values of "Europe", "China", and "India". You might also have products with a manufacturer's rating. For example, Intel processors. They all have a star rating from one to five. You could create a feature of colors. The important point here is that features are usually used when it is not a fundamental part of the buying decision.

When you create features and values, you assign them to appropriate products. PrestaShop very kindly creates an extra tab on the appropriate page with all the appropriate features and values. The customer might not bother checking these values so clearly; PrestaShop's **Features** is for additional information that the customer might want to read.

You probably wouldn't create a color feature for a T-shirt. That would be a critical or fundamental part of the buying decision and would almost certainly be in the product description, title, image, or attribute (more in a bit). However, the color of a computer cable would be a secondary or optional requirement and might make a good candidate for a feature.

One thing features are definitely not used for is when that feature makes a difference to the price. Variations like this would be handled by another aspect of PrestaShop that we will cover very soon. Also, features will not show as part of the description when added to the customer's cart. If this is important to you, then **Features** is not for you.

Think carefully about how PrestaShop's **Features** can be used for your product range and have a look at the quick manner in which you can implement them.

# Time for action – using PrestaShop's features

Here we will implement a range of features and values. I am using the country of origin example; you can choose what is appropriate to your product range.

1.  Click on **Catalog | Features**.

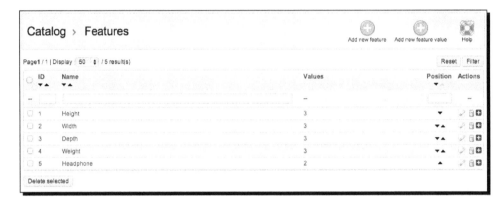

2.  Now click on **Add new feature** and type the name of your first feature and then click on **Save**.

3.  Next click on the **Add new feature value** button and type the name of the first value of this feature. Select from the drop-down list the new feature, and then click on **Save**.

4.  Repeat step 3 for all values of that feature.

5.  Repeat steps 2 and 3 for all of the features you want to create.

6.  Now click on the **Catalog** tab again and browse to the category of the first product you want to add a feature to. Click on the product to edit it.

7.  Now click on **Features**.

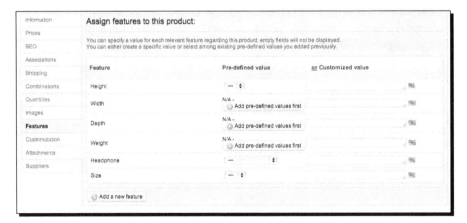

8. Select the feature and then the value from the drop-down list and click on **Save**.

9. Go and look at the cool **Data sheet** tab that has appeared with that product on the shop front.

10. Assign as many products and values as you need.

## What just happened?

You have now implemented the features option on your product range and have learned that features are for optional or additional product information that does not affect the price.

Now we can go on to explore and discuss product attributes. **Attributes** sounds fairly dull but in fact is a very powerful feature and in my opinion is probably better implemented in PrestaShop than in any other shopping cart software. This is because PrestaShop makes a potentially complicated process nice and simple.

# Attributes

These are a lot more interesting than the name suggests. PrestaShop allows you to create attribute groups and then actual attributes within those groups, and then assigns them to products. A very quick and simplistic way of describing an attribute would be as a product variation.

For example, attributes are a perfect way to have a single product: teddy T-shirt. Then create a **Color** attribute group and lots of actual attributes—**Red**, **Blue**, **Pink**, and so on. The customer could then, from one single product page, select any of the available colors for that teddy T-shirt. Have a look at attributes in action:

As you can see, the customer is able to click on a drop-down box and choose from the different attributes (product variations). The first thing to note here is that this is a simplistic example and we will get a bit deeper into this before we try attributes out. The other thing to point out is that just because you might sell a product with multiple variations does not mean you must have attributes.

As an example, I might introduce a range of teddy T-shirts with karate, heart, or skateboarder pictures. I certainly could create an attribute group called style and attribute values of karate, heart, and skateboarder. However, I might decide that displaying all of the styles and their pictures in a list in the teddy T-shirts' category was very important, perhaps to make sure that all the options were clearly visible. In this instance, using attributes wouldn't be a good idea.

So as with other product options in PrestaShop, attributes and their usage need to be considered and planned carefully. Always keep in mind what is best for helping the customer make a purchase!

I said that my example was simplistic. You can actually do so much with attributes that it is really not possible to cover it all in this book. Here are some of the most likely scenarios where attributes are indispensable.

What if my teddy T-shirts came in white, green, blue, and pink? Consider if the white version was £5 and all the colored versions were £7. This is no problem at all. I can create attributes and groups and specify the different increases in price that the different attributes should have. Then when the customer uses the drop-down menu to browse the different options, they would be presented with the correct price. Not only this but the product image can also be varied to show the different options as and when they are selected.

PrestaShop even allows you to specify a new weight for each combination (for shipping purposes), an eco-tax, and different references/barcodes for each variation. PrestaShop even has a "product combinations generator" to enable automatic assigning of specified attributes to any given product.

## Time for action – an attributes example

Here we will see how to create several versions of a product. The customer can then select the one they want from a drop-down list. The product price and images will also be updated:

1. Click on **Catalog** and then on **Attributes and Values**.

2. Let's start by adding an attribute. Click on **Add new Attributes** and type in the name of your attributes group. In my case, T-shirt styles.

3. Notice you have the option to enter a different public name. So you could call your attribute group something different in the admin and shop fronts. If this is important, perhaps to avoid using overly technical terms, then do so. If possible, I would keep them the same to avoid confusion.

4. Click on **Save** when you're ready.

5. Next click on **Add new value**. I will be adding my first T-shirt style—Karate. Then **Save** it. Keep adding attribute values from different groups until you have added all that you need.

6.  The color checkbox gives you the facility to provide actual colors, not just descriptions. If you choose these, you will simply enter a color code as well as an attribute value for each option. If you are providing an image for each attribute option, this feature is unnecessary. I suggest leaving it unchecked unless your situation specifically requires it.

7.  Now we will go to the first product that we need to add these newly created attributes to. So click on **Catalog**, find the appropriate product, and click on it to edit it.

8.  Notice the **Combinations** tab among the other product tabs. Click on it and we will create our product combinations from our attributes.

9.  At the top, click on new combination.

10. Below this click on **Add** and it will be added to the box. You can add multiple attributes to this product this way, but keep it simple for now and leave it at just one.

11. You can now optionally add references, locations, and EAN codes.

12. Here is the really good bit. Suppose one option is a bit more expensive, a bit heavier, or has a different eco-tax to the original product to be applied, simply enter that next in the area indicated below:

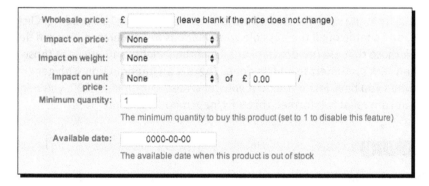

13. Enter an **Quantity**, or **Wholesale price** if it is different from the original product. When it comes to **Impact on price**, select **None**, **Increase** or **Decrease**, then in the quantity box put the amount of the increase or decrease. You can do the same with weight, but as explained when creating products, this is only necessary if you intend to calculate postage using weight.

14. If you want to create a different image for this combination, it needs to be previously uploaded on the image tab. You can then simply check the box next to the appropriate image.

15. When you're done, click on **Save**.

16. You can now click on the product again, select **Combinations** again, and add another combination based on different attributes.

17. Go and have a look at your product in the shop front to see it in action.

## What just happened?

You now know how to create product combinations using attributes.

The last possibility I would like you to just consider is this. Remember accessories? Your customers are shown a range of pre-selected add-on sales to choose from. What about creating attribute groups to match product categories and values to match actual products? Your customers could click on a drop-down menu and instantly add the T-shirt of their choice to their teddy. Nice!

## Have a go hero – the combinations generator

If like my teddy T-shirt example you only have a few combinations, that is not a problem. But what about if we had multiple combinations from multiple attribute groups each containing multiple values? The above process could be rather long and frustrating! Fortunately, there is a solution. The clue is in the *Have a go hero* title.

Here's the answer:

Simply click on the combinations generator at the top of the **Combinations** tab. Select all the attributes from the right-hand box that you want to use with this product. Click on **Add | Generate**, and a table of all the possible combinations are generated. You can delete with a single click those that are unnecessary and fill in the weights and prices of those you want to keep. Then click on **Generate** and its done. There is an imperfection with generating attributes when you have lots of them. If you generate more than 10,000, you might run into problems but I am reliably informed that a fix/new module is in progress.

# Customizing

This is a bit more niche than the other product features we have seen and there is a good chance you might not need this. But just knowing that you have the customizing option might open your mind to new ideas. And if you do need to offer your customer's custom options then this quick explanation and guide will be invaluable.

So what is customizing in a PrestaShop context? Click on the **Customization** tab of one of your products.

Notice you have the option to specify the number of **File fields** and/or **Text fields**. If you do, then these would appear on the product page. Try it if you're curious. So let's say I am selling a teddy bear T-shirt, and I would like the customer to specify a name to put on the T-shirt. All I need to do is to add a positive number in the appropriate box. PrestaShop would then pass on the details of the customization when the customer places the order. Of course, I could specify multiple text fields for a message. I could also specify a file field enabling the customer to upload a file to me. This could be a photograph for the teddy T-shirt or perhaps a picture to go on a custom gift tag.

All this assumes of course that I can produce the teddy T-shirts. PrestaShop obviously cannot do that for me. But the scope of the customization feature is only limited by your imagination. Here is a quick guide to add a customization to your product.

## Time for action – allowing your customers to customize

Follow this simple guide to add customizations to your products:

1.  Find and click on the product you want to add a customization option to.
2.  Click on the **Customization** tab and enter the number of file and text fields you require to enable your customers to configure their customization.
3.  Save the product.
4.  Go and visit the product page to see the effect. How simple was that?

### What just happened?

Although not needed by every store owner, this is a powerful product feature that is well worth being aware of.

## Product mania!

Everything we have looked at in this chapter is fairly non-technical. But the huge range of options and features you have at your disposal can sometimes cause apparent complexity. It is well worth playing with the PrestaShop catalog options, and perhaps, re-reading this chapter so that you can fully grasp how PrestaShop manages your catalog and how incredibly flexible and diverse it is.

Having said that, don't hold back on further development until everything is perfect. Any e-commerce store should be an ongoing cyclical thing that you constantly add to, improve, and refine. Also, don't forget my suggestion about opening your shop with just a core range of products and then adding more on an ongoing basis. If you can be making money while working on your catalog, then I think it makes sense.

## Pop quiz – a few product marketing questions

Q1. Using what you have just learned, how could you sell a product for less than the cost price and still make a profit on the purchase?

- By looking for a cheaper supplier
- By Creating a special offer
- By setting the price very high at first and later on, drop the price

Q2. Arrange the following into feature, advantage, and benefit:

- Women will love you
- Your abs will be rock solid
- The new body toner uses the latest fitness technology

# Summary

We learned a lot in this chapter about e-merchandising. You now have well-presented products with descriptions that actually sell.

Specifically, we covered:

- Categories: We learned about planning, structure, creation, and describing them in an enticing manner.
- Products: We saw how to create and implement them as well as creating short, concise sales copy that sells.
- Product options: We looked at a whole range of ways to enhance, highlight, and offer options on your products, including special offers, linking accessories, attributes, recently viewed, and offering customization.

Now that your products are ready, it is time to look at the rest of the content of your site and how to give more to your customers and how to get more customers. This topic will be covered in the next chapter.

# 4

# Getting More Customers

*In this chapter, we will be looking at a number of topics related to getting more visitors to your website. There are two main ways in which we can achieve this. The first is by giving in to the whims of the search engines. We will look at keywords; everything from choosing them to using them, and taking advantage of a whole range of PrestaShop SEO (Search Engine Optimization) utilities.*

*We will also look at giving your customers a bit more. Your potential customers' visit to your site needs to be worthwhile and useful for them. We will achieve this by talking about writing articles related to your business and then we will use the PrestaShop content management features to highlight them.*

We will look at a few really quick and simple methods to attract customers who speak a language that is different ours. We will look at the following features:

- Choosing the best keywords
- Making food for the search engines
- Refining PrestaShop search
- Tag clouds
- Using the PrestaShop CMS
- URLs in PrestaShop
- Robots and sitemaps
- Using PrestaShop language features

So let's get on with it.

# SEO: Search Engine Optimization

It is my opinion that people are more important than search engines when marketing your content. It's true, though, that there are lots of things you can and cannot do to try and improve your success with search engines regarding the number of visitors that they send you.

You can read enormous technical books written by greatly esteemed gurus on the subject, but consider this: search engine companies invest vast fortunes in their systems; they do this so that they can present to their users interesting, useful, and (here's the big one) appropriate content based on the search their user performs.

Therefore, by understanding your customer, your business, and your product niche, you will achieve far more than by using any trick or secret that can be shared in a book. The important questions for us now are, how well do we understand our customers and which keywords and search terms will our customers use?

## Which keywords should we use?

Are you using the same keywords and phrases your customers will be using? Let us assume that you are selling big television sets, and throughout your website you refer to them as "flat panel TVs". Is that the most popular phrase the type of person you are trying to attract will use to search for your product?

If people don't search for "flat panel TVs", and instead use the terms "plasma screen", "LCD TV", "OLED television", or one of dozens of other phrases with a similar meaning, you will miss out on loads of free visitors. What about this conundrum—laptop, notebook, or portable PC? That is the question; how would you decide?

There are a number of premium software programs and web services you can buy, but I am guessing you didn't buy this book just to be referred to someone else for an additional expense. There are various sites where you can get a limited time trial of products that will help you find the popular keywords for your industry. Later, in *Chapter 9, Go...to the Future* we will look at Google Analytics, which has precise tools for choosing keywords.

But as optimization is an ongoing process, I don't recommend even the free ones, as you will have to pay eventually. And Google Analytics, although free, does not give you the hands-on experience and feedback that you will get by following this guide. Now if you are building a PrestaShop megastore with thousands of products, then fine, get your wallet out. Otherwise try this.

## Discovering the value of keywords

Visit Google, Bing, and the other search engines, and search for different terms. Keep it simple. Perhaps just two or three word phrases to start with. If there are a couple of paid-for adverts down the right-hand side or at the top, then you have probably chosen a phrase that is worth considering. I say this because the fact that there is an advert means that somebody else believes it is worth paying for. It is not necessary to have the best phrase; innovate, create, and you might discover a phrase that a lot of people in your industry would be prepared to pay for.

Different niches will have different volumes of competition, so you have to compare the phrases for your niche to others. Next, search for the same terms again and take a look at the number of results returned for that search. Be sure to have a pen and paper handy to make notes on your findings.

# Meta tags

Meta tags are words and descriptions about the information on your PrestaShop shop that are not seen by your customer. They reside in the code of your page, which some search engines read to help determine the words that they will use to index your site. Implementing meta tags well could help the search engines accurately determine your site's content. Meta tags are not as important as they used to be—some search engines do not use them at all—but they are so simple to implement in PrestaShop that they are well worth using.

They should be a part of your overall keyword strategy; we've already taken a look at them.

Meta tags can be defined for PrestaShop category, product, and article pages. Here I will show you how to easily add them to your category and product pages, and you will see how to add them to your articles later in the chapter.

## Types of meta tags

There are meta titles, meta descriptions, and meta keywords. We will start with a brief explanation of each type of meta tag, then a *Time for action* section where you can begin to implement them.

- ◆ **Meta titles** are short titles relevant to the specific page concerned. If this is an article, then the meta title can be the same as the title. If the page is a category or product, then a bit more imagination could be worthwhile. Perhaps a 50 cm tall fluffy teddy with extra fluff could become "Buy this 50 cm fluffy teddy with extra fluff finish".

♦ **Meta descriptions** are easy to define for products and categories. Often the brief descriptions from the product pages are suitable here. For articles, a brief summary of the title and key points would be good.

♦ **Meta keywords** are lists of keywords you deem the most appropriate for use on any given page—just one, two, or three word phrases separated by a comma in a list. For example, fluffy teddy, teddies, extra fluff, 50 cm teddy bear, and so on.

# Time for action – PrestaShop meta tags

This section shows you where and how to enter your meta information for products and categories. Articles are covered later in the chapter.

*1.* Hover on the **Catalog** tab and click on **Categories**, and then click on the **Edit** icon of the first category to add meta tags. Scroll down to the meta information text boxes and enter your meta tags. Save the category.

*2.* Repeat the first step until all your categories have meta tags.

*3.* Hover on the **Catalog** tab and then click on **Products** then click on the first product that you want to add meta tags to. Click on the **SEO** tab on the left-hand side panel and enter your meta tags. Save the product.

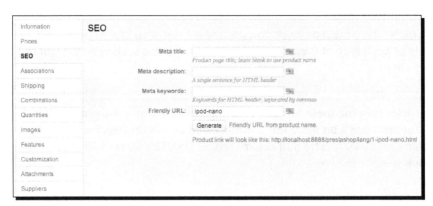

**4.** Repeat until all your products have meta tags.

## What just happened?

Your products and categories now have meta information so that (some) search engines can quickly assess the likely content of your website.

# Tag clouds

Tag clouds are cool. They look good, the search engines like them, and customers like them. But what are they? A tag cloud is a list of keywords and phrases arranged in a way so as to tempt visitors to click on them. But why would we do this? What is the point?

It doesn't matter how well you define your meta tags or how carefully you write your product descriptions and articles. Some visitors might still turn up on your website, by accident.

A tag cloud is a bit like an unordered, highly relevant index. It contains the words and phrases you choose. So visitors scan the words (because that is what their brains do) and if they see a word or phrase that means something to them, they click it. And hey presto, they are on the relevant product page that has all the information they need. That's the theory anyway.

Actually, a tag cloud can seriously enhance your site's usability and profitability. Here is one from www.amazon.com:

If you want your own tag cloud, read on.

## Time for action – creating a tag cloud

Let's see how to create a tag cloud.

1. Click on the **Modules** subtab under the **Modules** tab and scroll down to the **Tags block** module.

2. Now click on **Configure**.

3. Here you can choose the number of tags you want there to be in your cloud. There is no best number as such, just choose what is right for your shop. For instance, for a small PrestaShop online store that I had made with 10 products, a cloud of 10 tags looked good and some really relevant tags were displayed.

4. Play with the number of tags and see what is displayed and what your tag cloud looks like on your shop front. Click on **Save** each time you try a different number.

### What just happened?

You just made your shop front a lot more friendly. A tag cloud is great for those of your visitors who do a one-click search. And lots of visitors who won't use a search box will use a tag cloud.

# Friendly URLs

A friendly URL is the best way to remember a web address; the customer can easily revisit a website by typing this in the address bar. In PrestaShop, a friendly URL will be in the format `domain/category/product.`

## Time for action – how to get search-friendly URLs

So there are big benefits for completing this *Time for action*. We need to make a minor modification to the files on our website and then tell PrestaShop to enable friendly URLs. Here goes:

1. Hover over the **Preferences** tab then click on **SEO & URLs**.

2. Scroll down, select **Yes** on **Friendly URL**, and click on **Save**.

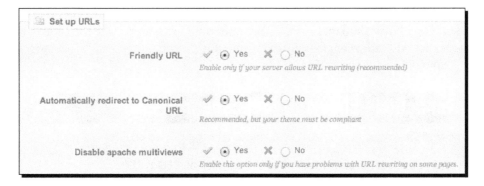

3. On the dashboard, you can check whether everything went smoothly.

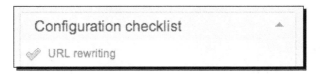

4. Now, it is possible that this didn't work! It is even possible that you get an error whenever you try to view your store. Don't panic. This means that your web host does not support URL rewriting. Simply go back to Step 2 and disable friendly URLs, and all will be well. A web host not supporting URL rewriting seems to be a fairly rare event these days, so it is very unlikely that this will be a problem.

## What just happened?

First of all, when you click on the **Save** button, PrestaShop creates a file on your website that gives instructions to the Apache web server to dig deeper; this file is called `.htaccess`. This then enables PrestaShop to make use of a web server feature called URL rewriting. PrestaShop uses this to make up friendly URLs. We also mentioned that if your web host does not allow its server to do this, then you will need to disable the friendly URL feature.

# Canonical URLs

Canonical URLs refer to when similar or duplicate content appears on your website, but on different URLS. The simplest explanation is `www.yoursite.com` and `yoursite.com`. Type either of these into a web browser and you will probably end up on your home page. This apparently harmless situation can cause problems with how highly search engines rate your page.

When you specify your preferred canonical URL as either www.yoursite.com or yoursite.com, PrestaShop makes minor but important modifications to the code in your web pages that tells search engines what the situation on your website is. This helps avoid any of the pitfalls mentioned earlier.

## Time for action – choosing your canonical URL

Here's how to specify your canonical URL and tell PrestaShop to use it:

1. Hover over the **Preferences** tab and then click on **SEO & URLs**.
2. Now scroll down to the **Set up URLs** section.
3. Click on **Yes** for **Automatically redirect to Canonical URL**.
4. Click on **Save**, and you're done.

### What just happened?

PrestaShop will now make sure that your chosen canonical URL is used exclusively. This, as we discussed, has great potential benefits for the search engine ranking of your site. Now let's take a look at adding some great articles to your PrestaShop store.

# Writing and displaying articles

Articles are what you give to people as an incentive to visit your website, especially when they are not considering a purchase. By creating high quality, useful articles, you can attract visitors through search engines, create loyalty, and subtly promote products.

## Good ideas when writing articles

Most of your visitors are probably not planning on reading all of your articles or even a single page. They are most likely looking for a fact, figure, or piece of information.

The goal is to make it very easy for them to find and even more compelling to continue reading.

## Make your articles easy to read

Reading from a screen is more difficult than reading from a book. That is why you need to consider making readability as high as possible when writing your articles. If you have a subject people are interested in (which you will find out when they visit repeatedly) and you focus your efforts in making your pages easy to get information from, then people will like your articles. And if we work on the assumption that search engines know what people want, they will also rank you higher and more sites will want to link to you. The result is more visitors. So by focusing on what your visitor wants, you will get what *you* want.

Consider carefully who your website and the specific page you are working on are aimed at. Under what circumstances would somebody want to read your page? Is the page worded and structured in such a way as to accommodate their circumstances? Do the most important pieces of information jump out of the page or are they hidden away in a huge section in the middle?

## Think about your audience

Think about the level of expertise your customers have. What language or level of industry jargon will they like and what will bore them? Don't use technical jargon or clever words unless you are certain that is what your reader likes.

Don't use long words where short ones will do. Forget about preamble! Your first heading and paragraph should be 100 percent specific and lay out clearly what the rest of the article is about. By all means use colorful and interesting language, but not at the expense of immediate clarity. The first heading should sum up the article; for example, you would put "How to write articles" first and not "Hints and tips when getting started with writing".

## Sell, but sell subtly

Don't go over the top. Don't give away the product. It is perfectly acceptable to turn a word or phrase in your article into a link to a product, as long as it doesn't trick the reader into viewing the product; but don't use too many product links. Links to information the reader is looking for are the most important, or readers might find your web page too hard to navigate, and leave. Don't forget that the article is surrounded by your PrestaShop modules—new products, specials, and so on. They will find your products when they are ready to.

Don't promote your products unless it is appropriate. In every industry, there are products that are right for different people in different situations. If you are a 100 percent honest when you are in a situation where your product is not suitable, your reader will subconsciously recognize your honesty.

If you recommend a cheap, reliable laptop that is appropriate for a student, and if that recommendation seems fit to him/her, you might get a recommendation. Also, when you explain how wonderful and appropriate another product is, they are more likely to believe you and get their wallet out.

## Page formatting and keyword density

Headers, underlines, italics, image filenames, article titles, and so on—that's what formatting is. It's all the different ways in which you can present information or add relevance and appropriateness to the article.

Use relevant keywords and phrases to name your pictures and pages. For example, use `15cm_fluffy_teddy.jpg` instead of `img012.jpg`.

Focus your effort on what is good for humans. Create an H2 heading containing the keywords/phrases at the beginning of the article. Use the same keywords/phrases in the first paragraph. Consider making them bold or italicized. Use H3 and H4 headings generously and appropriately, with similar or identical keywords/phrases later in the article. Lots of well-ordered, clear, nested headings make your articles easily scanable and more likely to be read in full.

Use links (with keywords/phrases) to relevant parts of the same page or other pages in your shop. All the above techniques not only make your article easier to scan, but they also highlight key bits of information, making your article genuinely useful. When you make useful articles, visitors will like you, and people buy from people they like.

## How many times should the keywords/phrases be used?

This is probably one of the most widely sought after pieces of information on SEO. What percentage of keyword density is perfect? That is, if your page has a hundred words, how many of them are the words you think people searching for you will use?

In a nutshell: sorry, I don't know. If you take Google for example, their formula for calculating page rank is a very closely guarded secret. If somebody tells you the percentage is "x", then they are lying, misinformed, or at best, making an estimate based on experience.

The truth is that there probably is no specific percentage anyway. It is, in fact, based on a publicly unknown and extremely complicated list of variables like the number of links to your site, their content, the rank of the site, the pages they appear on, the density, spacing, format, and their location on the page, as well as the location of the page on your site, and many more factors.

So how on earth do you optimize for such complexity? The most important thing you can do is make sure you choose the words your customers are likely to use. Use them in different formats and locations: headings, links, underlines, bold, and so on. Some should be near the end of the page, some in the links outside the main body of the page, and some in the pages linking to the page.

However, do not use more keywords or phrases than is natural to a human reader. If it sounds natural, looks natural, and uses the words and phrases your customers are using, that's good.

# Quick tips

- If you have a complicated subject where you need to go into detail, then that's not a problem. Try to keep the beginning of the article simple and build the complexity later in the article, and pay extra attention to all the rest of the tips.

- Think and plan the structure of your article before you start writing. This includes deciding upon highly relevant, to-the-point titles and subtitles. Good and frequent subtitles divide your article into sections and help readers target what they want, and this makes the whole article easier to read.

- Use shorter paragraphs and sentences. They make your article easier to read.

- Use bulleted lists for key pieces of information. A bit like these.

- Don't make the pages too long. Consider breaking the article into multiple articles if it seems heavy to read it all together.

Most readers will scan the first line of a few titles and paragraphs to discover if your article has what they want. Make the first sentence of each paragraph highly relevant and precise.

# Writing the summary

Everything discussed in the preceding sections might seem a bit daunting, but try to write your articles keeping all that guidance in mind, but don't wait until it is perfect. You wouldn't be reading this now if I had aimed for perfection. Is it useful? Is it clear and simple to scan and read? Is it professional? If so, publish it. You can always revise it another time or react to feedback.

# Using the CMS

Now that we have gone through the ins and outs of writing good articles for your website, it is time to actually put up those articles on your website. If you have the articles at hand, ready to be copied and pasted, that's great! If you like, you can write them as you go. Remember the tip about not waiting until it's perfect?

## Time for action – creating the article

Let's use the CMS to create your first article on PrestaShop.

1. Hover over the **Preferences** tab and then click on **CMS**.

2. Click on the first green button, **Add new**, in **CMS Categories** . This is how we will create a new CMS Category.

3. Fill in all the required fields.

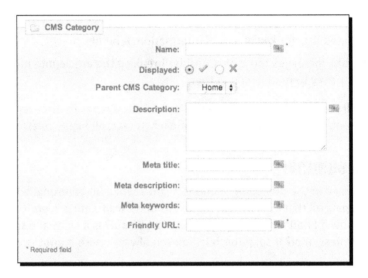

4. You now know exactly what to do with the three "meta" options.

5. Friendly URLs are cool. I suggest you enter the title of your article in this field, with a dash between each word. So `Why teddies are so fluffy` would be entered as `why-teddies-are-so-fluffy`. Just leave out the speech marks and use lower case for all the characters.

6. Select the **Parent CMS Category**.

7. Click on **Save**. Now you have a new CMS category.

8. Now click on the **Add new** button next to **Pages in this category**.

**9.** Fill all the required fields.

**10.** Don't forget to select the **Displayed** option, otherwise your new article will not be readable.

**11.** When the article is ready, click on **Save**.

**12.** Repeat these steps as many times as you want to write new articles.

## What just happened?

You have written an article and put it on the PrestaShop system. There is just one thing left to be done. How can people read your article?

# robots.txt

Search engines are our guests. They should be looked after and treated respectfully, because when they get grumpy with you they can cause all sorts of problems. For example, they could stop sending you visitors. Never forget that search engines are businesses themselves. They are not obliged to feature you in their search results.

Creating a file and placing it conveniently on your website server will let the search engines know that they are welcome, but you also need to point out that there are some places that a guest should not go. That's fine, they won't be offended. In fact, they will be quite pleased that you saved them the bother of searching areas that are not needed. Want to see what `robots.txt` looks like? Have a look at the following screenshot or download your copy of the file from the main, top-level folder of your website:

```
 9    User-agent: *
10    # Private pages
11    Disallow: /*orderby=
12    Disallow: /*orderway=
13    Disallow: /*tag=
14    Disallow: /*id_currency=
15    Disallow: /*search_query=
16    Disallow: /*back=
17    Disallow: /*utm_source=
18    Disallow: /*utm_medium=
19    Disallow: /*utm_campaign=
```

You can see that the `robots.txt` file is not like brain surgery; moreover, there are many things you can do with one. For a full exploration of `robots.txt` files, have a look at `www.robotstxt.org`, or to quickly generate the recommended PrestaShop default, complete the following *Time for action* section.

# Time for action – creating robots.txt

Here, we will create a `robots.txt` file and place it on your web server. It will keep the search engines from indexing unnecessary pages like account pages. This is good, as it will prevent search results about your site from becoming cluttered.

1. In your PrestaShop control panel, hover over the **Preferences** tab and click on **SEO & URLs**.
2. Scroll down to the **Robots file generation** section.
3. Click on the **Generate robots.txt file** button.
4. Now you have a `robots.txt` file on your server.

# What just happened?

You have just (respectfully) marked a few areas of your store as off-limits to the search engines. However, please note this is not a security feature. It does not block access, but merely asks search engines (99 percent of them) to avoid certain areas. We will cover actual security measures in *Chapter 6, Security and Disaster Recovery*.

# Helping Google with sitemaps

A sitemap is just that—a map. It outlines the structure of your website and includes pertinent information such as the date on which it was last updated and the frequency with which it is updated. Suppose that you added an important product to the bottom of a big subcategory. In all likelihood, Google will have to crawl through your entire site to find it and add it to the search results.

With sitemaps, Google can be made aware of this page, any other such pages, and any modifications. Google can then specifically crawl the new or updated pages. This is better for you and easier for Google.

## Time for action – Google sitemaps tutorial

So how do we get one of these `sitemap.xml` files? You probably guessed. PrestaShop has a module that makes one. And as always it's a breeze to implement.

1.  Click on the **Modules** subtab under the **Modules** tab and scroll down to the **Google sitemap** module.

2.  Click on **Configure**.

3.  To generate the `sitemaps.xml` file after you have selected your options, click on the **Update sitemap file** button.

4.  You should do this every time you add to your site, such as adding products, categories, or articles. Also, do this if you're making a significant change to the content as well.

5.  Want to have a look what this `sitemap.xml` file looks like? Click on the link that the Google sitemap module displays. Have a look at all the information that PrestaShop has generated.

## What just happened?

Creating and keeping this file up-to-date will help Google easily keep up with the changes to your website, and that is a good thing. You can also consider submitting a sitemap to Yahoo! and Bing.

# PrestaShop search weightings

So how does the PrestaShop search system work? It works in much the same way as a real search engine. It analyzes the content of the shop and matches it to the words and phrases used by your visitors when they type in a search query. It then uses *weightings*, a sort of important criterion, to decide which results to give to the visitor.

The criteria considered include category, product, article, and even meta tags. So which is most important? PrestaShop does know what it is doing (trust me on that) and it has devised default weightings for each type of content. As you might expect with PrestaShop, these weightings are configurable. To get an idea of how it works, have a look at the next screenshot or log in to your PrestaShop control panel, hover over the **Preferences** tab, and click on **Search**.

Let's run through the options. At the top of the **Search** section, you have a **Yes** or **No** option for **Ajax search**. This refers to the cool manner in which the search results are displayed as you type. If you think your customers are likely to be using old web browsers or you are using one of the older PrestaShop templates discussed in *Chapter 2, Back Office*, then you can choose **No**. Otherwise, you might as well leave it on **Yes** for the user-friendly and rather nifty effects.

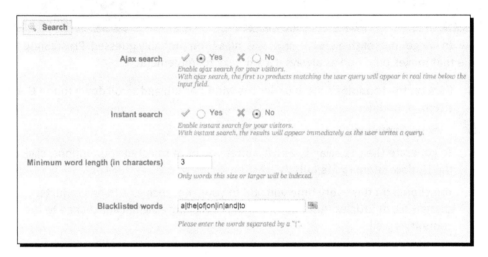

**Instant search** is a functionality that allows the autocomplete feature for the search field. This can be useful for your visitors.

**Minimum word length (in characters)** is just what the name says. You can define a minimum word length for PrestaShop to start bothering with the identification of words. Three is a good minimum, so words like "at", "a", "is", and "by" are ignored. This is almost always a good idea.

The next option, **Blacklisted words**, allows you to specifically name a list of words that you want ignored. If you sold products like c5, then you would obviously need to allow two-letter words in your search results. You could then specifically define the two-letter words you didn't want included here, such as "at", "a", "is", and "by".

The next section contains a list of content areas, and boxes to type in your chosen weight for each content area. The higher the number, the more important that content area is considered. Now that you know how to change the weightings, do consider that PrestaShop developers know what they are doing, but they might not know what you are doing. That is why I have brought these search options to your attention. As usual, think and plan what is important on your sites, and make changes if needed.

---

🔍 **Weight**

The "weight" represents its importance and relevance for the ranking of the products when try a new search.
A word with a weight of 8 will have 4 times more value than a word with a weight of 2.

That's why we advise to set a greater weight for words which appear in the name or reference of a product than the ones in the description. Thus, the search results will be as precise and relevant as possible.

| | |
|---|---|
| Product name weight | 6 |
| Reference weight | 10 |
| Short description weight | 1 |
| Description weight | 1 |
| Category weight | 3 |
| Manufacturer weight | 3 |
| Tags weight | 4 |
| Attributes weight | 2 |
| Features weight | 2 |

# Switching languages

This is great. PrestaShop has very helpfully created versions of its software in many languages. Your first option is to download and install PrestaShop in the language of your choice. Here I am assuming that you have already downloaded and set up PrestaShop in your language, but you now want to add another.

Because PrestaShop has already done the work to make it available in so many languages, it is quite easy to add another language. But what do I mean by adding another language? All the content that you create remains the same. But all the default writing can be changed by the customer to any language that you choose to allow them to install. What this means is that all your blocks, modules, buttons, checkout instructions, and more, will change languages at the click of a button.

In some cases, this will be enough to get a sale from somebody who speaks that other language, but that is not always the case. We will go a little further with the next tutorial. For now, here's how to allow your customers to change the default language in the shop front.

## Time for action – enabling a second language

It is very simple to vary the following instructions to install whichever language you want:

1. Hover over the **Localization** tab, click on **Languages**, and then click on the **Add new** button.

2. Now fill the form. The name should be straightforward, for example, **French**, **German**, **Swahili**, or whatever.

3. Every country has an internationally recognized country code. To find the one for your second language, visit `http://www.iso.org/iso/country_codes/`. Enter this in the **ISO code** box.

4. Next, for the **Flag** field, browse to a graphic of the flag for that country. A handy website very helpfully makes some available here: `http://www.famfamfam.com/lab/icons/flags/`. Upload it and move on.

5. In the **"No-picture" image** box, you will need to provide a graphic that PrestaShop will use when no product image is available. If you always provide an image, this can be anything. If you regularly have missing pictures, a "picture coming soon" in the language you are enabling will suffice.

6. Make sure there is a nice green tick for the **Status** setting, and then click on **Save**.

7. But PrestaShop cannot speak another language yet! We need to download a language pack from PrestaShop. The language packs are on the same page as the main PrestaShop download. Go grab your language pack(s) now from `http://www.PrestaShop.com/en/downloads/`.

8. Now hover over **Localization** tab and click on the **Localization**. In the **Import localization pack** section, browse to the language pack you just downloaded and click on **Import**.

9. Click on the **Languages** subtab again and make sure your new language is enabled.

10. Now click on the **Modules** subtab, scroll down to **Language block**, and install it.

11. Visit your shop front. Notice that you have some little flags that enable your customers to choose their preferred language. It is important that you explore your shop front in detail. How widely used your new language is might depend upon the extent to which the language pack covers all aspects of your shop. Any translations that have not been done and any extra translations that you would like to be done for your site are talked about in the next guide.

## What just happened?

You just went global! Well, sort of. If your language pack did not translate everything you wanted, it is not the end of the world. If your product is niche enough, you might still get some sales. If you need to translate even more, then read on.

Now we can go on and explore how to add more translations for key parts of your PrestaShop.

# Creating translations

To see the extent of the translations so far, hover over the **Localization** tab, click on **Translations**, and in the box labeled **Modify translations**, select the area that you want to translate and click on the flag of your new language. Now go to the section that you want translated and click on **Expand all fieldsets**, or choose a specific one. You will be able to see a complete list of all the translations.

For many languages, there are upwards of 500 translations that can be done for you—an example of the power of the open source community. Imagine the cost of paying someone to translate just a few languages. PrestaShop gives it to you for nothing and you don't even have to say thanks.

Notice that on this page, you can easily add or change the translations. However, there is one very significant area that is not translated at all! That is our product descriptions. The next *Time for action* section will show you how to do this. But before we dive in, let's look at how to translate from our native language to a new language.

Perhaps (obviously) it would be helpful if you have somebody who speaks both languages. But assuming that you don't, and you don't want to get your wallet out, here is a cheap, not totally reliable, but potentially profitable trick.

Please note that we will be using a translation service that is free but not totally accurate. If you are translating something where inaccuracy could cause a problem, don't use this method. For example, it is probably okay to risk details of a teddy bear getting mixed up in translation, but the firing instructions for a new range of rocket-propelled grenades would clearly be problematic.

After this guide, I will point out how this very simple method can be used to translate almost all aspects of your PrestaShop store.

# Time for action – translating product descriptions

1. Log in to your PrestaShop back office.

2. Hover over the **Catalog** tab and find the first product that you would like to translate. Click on the **Edit** icon and then click on the flag next to the **Title** box. Notice that since we've added a new language, you have an extra option to change the language.

3. Now we need to redo all the description and title fields in our new language. Let's go over and use Google Translate to help us. Visit `http://translate.google.com/`.

4. Select your "from" and "to" languages in the drop-down box, and copy and paste, individually, the descriptions and titles you want translated. Click on **Translate**, and copy and paste the translations back into their respective fields on the PrestaShop product page. A quick tip: as already mentioned, this is far from perfect. Consider shortening and simplifying the product descriptions. Click on **Save** when you're done.

5. Go and look at your shop front, change the setting to your new language, and check out the product description.

## What just happened?

When we saved the product, PrestaShop kept the original product information and descriptions as well as all the new information and descriptions we provided for the new language. PrestaShop will show customers the product description relevant to their choice of language.

What is important to realize is that if you see a flag anywhere on your PrestaShop site, you can click on it and add a translation. Also, meta tags, categories, and even whole articles in the CMS can have translations added in this way.

You might be wondering why we should settle for such imperfection. Some would say amateurism, simply because it works and it costs nothing to try. If you find you are getting significant numbers of customers from a particular country, then it might be time to show proper respect to their language and get your wallet out. Visit `www.elance.com` and check out their outsourcing website. You often get great deals on translation. But beware. There are great translators and not-so-great translators.

## Time for action – translating your whole website

Here's how to do it:

1. Revisit your home page via Google Translate. Highlight and copy the URL of your translated home page.

2. Click on the **Modules** subtab and scroll down to the **Home text editor** module. Click on **Configure**.

3. At the very top of your home page, add the flag of the language of your choice. Now highlight the flag in the editor and click on the link button.

4. Paste the translated URL into the box shown below the labeled **Link URL**.

5. Save your new home page and visit your shop front to try it out.

### What just happened?

Your customers can now switch to a completely translated version of your store. You can, of course, offer buttons for multiple language options.

## Languages conclusion

As previously discussed, if you want to be successful with one or more new languages, it might be worth paying for professional translation. But why not go one stage further? If you find you have tapped a lucrative market in another country, why not start a website hosted in that country, with a domain extension specific to that country, which uses their language primarily? Have a look at *Chapter 9, Go... to the Future* and read about duplication, if this is of interest to you.

## Pop quiz – PrestaShop search

Q1. If you have a range of products, say teddy bears, and you want to make sure that the search results for teddy bear show at the top, and you want this page to list all the teddies in the teddy category (and not just individual teddy pages), how would you do this?

1. By adding tags to every product under the teddy category.

2. By setting weights in the **Search** section under the **Preferences** tab.

3. Creating a sitemap file and linking it with Google Webmaster Tools.

Q2. How does the `robots.txt` file protect the private areas of your PrestaShop store?

1.   Adding the following line to the file: `Disallow: [Path]`.

2.   It is not possible to do this with `robots.txt`; the changes have to be done in PrestaShop.

3.   Adding the following line to the file: `NoAllow: [Path]`.

# Summary

You might be getting quite excited about your new PrestaShop store. The features and procedures that you have completed in this chapter together make for a very significantly optimized store. I have seen countless web stores, even some of the big names, that do not have anything like the SEO options that you now have enabled.

Now, this doesn't mean that this alone will suddenly bring a flood of visitors; it doesn't work like that. I can guarantee you that you have taken the very significant initial steps towards having a store that is approved of by humans and search engines alike. And in a later chapter, we will turn on the tap to begin the eventual flood of visitors. SEO should definitely be an ongoing project and I recommend further reading. A good place to start is a website that discusses SEO in a specifically PrestaShop context. Check out `www.presto-changeo.com` and have a look at some of the SEO tips and tricks. Also visit the PrestaShop forum at `www.PrestaShop.com` where they have a section dedicated to all things PrestaShop and SEO.

Specifically, we covered:

*   Choosing the best keywords: Deciding on an overall keyword strategy
*   Meta tags: What they are and how to benefit from them
*   URLs: All about canonical and friendly URLs
*   Writing and displaying great articles
*   Other SEO stuff: Aliases, sitemaps, `robots.txt`, and search weightings
*   Adding new languages to our PrestaShop site

Now it is time to look at more customization options as well as some of the lesser-spotted PrestaShop features, but let's talk about that in the next chapter.

# 5
# Tools, Newsletters, Extra Income, and Statistics

*In this chapter we will cover as many PrestaShop features as possible. As I mentioned earlier, there is so much to PrestaShop. This is an attempt to bring the best of it to your attention.*

*First we will explore the Preferences and Advanced Parameters tabs and then go on to some more great stuff like newsletters and product notifications. Then we will look at Google AdSense. This is a way of making extra income through advertisers with just a couple of clicks.*

*Then we will take our first look at statistics. I would say our first look because we will just introduce the concept and set them up. In Chapter 9, Go... To the Future, we will see how to start using the statistics you gather. We will set up the fabulously rich PrestaShop statistics features and the free-to-use Google Analytics.*

In this chapter, we are going to:

- Look at the most useful things on the **Preferences** tab
- Explore the best stuff on the **Advanced Parameters** tab
- Set up a newsletter and notifications system
- Talk about running an e-mail marketing campaign
- Set up PrestaShop statistics
- Set up Google Analytics

So let's get on with it...

# Exploring the Preferences tab

The options available under **Preferences** are very diverse. Some you might never want to use while others might work wonders for your business.

Next is a whirlwind tour of some of the options under **Preferences**. Each option described tells you quickly where it is and what it does. For brevity, I have left a few lesser (in my opinion) options out, and for sanity, I will not mention any that we have already looked at. So here we go...

## Useful preferences

These are the best things you will find under the **Preferences** tab that have not been covered already and will not be covered later in the book.

### General

If you want to give an extra security to your website and your web hosting has an SSL certificate, then you can enable it here and increase the front office security.

Also you can enable a multistore like we saw previously in the *Chapter 2, Back Office*.

### Orders

Here you could set up the orders through a five-step process, by default, or you could choose a shorter way to do a checkout only in one step.

Also here you can set up a minimum purchase, guest checkout, or gift-wrapping.

### Cart redisplay at login

What if PrestaShop could remember customers who had products in their cart, but didn't buy those products? This sounds like a good idea to me because you might get a sale from it. This functionality is in **Customers** under the **Preferences** tab

### Store contacts

Fill out all the contact details for your store. PrestaShop will automatically add relevant information accordingly.

# E-mail

The settings on this subtab are usually best left alone. The default settings of **Use PHP mail() function** and **Both** are typical to almost all shared hosting environments. If, however, you were running your PrestaShop from a server on your PC at home, you could choose **Set my own SMTP parameters** and configure PrestaShop to use your ISPs e-mail service and your own e-mail address. When hosting with a professional host, you could also use the SMTP service provided by your web host, but in most situations, this would be an unnecessary complication.

Leaving the **Both** option selected will give your customers the choice of receiving simple text e-mails or formatted HTML e-mails.

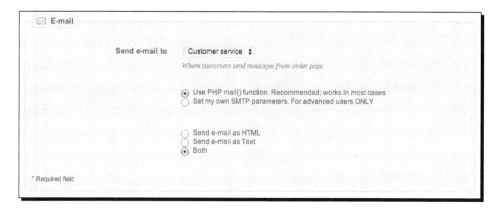

# Image

Use these settings to customize the look and feel of your store.

# Localization

Choose `lbs`, `kg`, or any other unit of measurement that suits you.

# Maintenance

If you need to fix something in your shop, probably you will need to activate this.

# Administration

Every tool has either been covered or will be covered in a specific section of the book. However, there are two tools that don't fall in any appropriate topic category. They are great for personalizing and customizing your admin control panel. These are **Menus** and **Quick Access**.

## Menus

Do you feel some of the tabs are in the wrong place? No problem. You can move and create as many tabs and subtabs as you like. So if you want to group different subtabs under different main tabs because that is convenient for you, then this is how to do it.

## Time for action – customizing your tabs

As an example, we will move the main **Orders** tab and make it a subtab of **Customers**:

1. Click on **Administration** and then on **Menus**.

2. Click on the edit icon under **Actions** for the **Orders** tab in the **Name** list.

3. We are going to change the **Parent** value from **Catalog** to **Customers**. This means that the **Orders** tab will be moved to a subtab of **Customers** instead of **Catalog** (a main tab). So click on the drop-down list and select **Customers**.

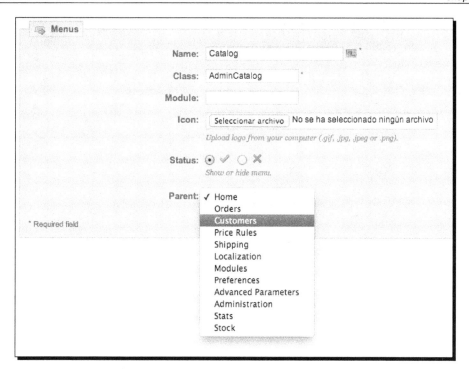

**4.** That's it. Click on the **Customers** tab and then on the newly positioned **Orders** tab. Notice that all the subtabs of **Orders** have moved with it. That is because although you have only moved the **Orders** tab, it remains the parent for all its subtabs.

## What just happened?

This feature might not be of any use to you. But imagine your business grows and you need to employ someone to perform one specific task. Perhaps you will need someone to write articles or do all the customer service and packing. In that case, you can easily create a single tab with all the features they need and then restrict their username to only that particular tab. This would avoid the risk of them accidentally changing settings (which you don't want them to). We will look at this and other security features in *Chapter 6, Security and Disaster Recovery*.

## Quick access

Remember the quick access drop-down list? Do they go where you want them to? Here is how to make more. I will make a quick access to the database backup facility, which we will use in the next chapter while making a copy of your store.

# Time for action – creating a Quick access

Here is how to do it:

1. Click on the **Administration** tab and then on **Quick Access**.

2. Now click on the **Add new** button (with the + sign).

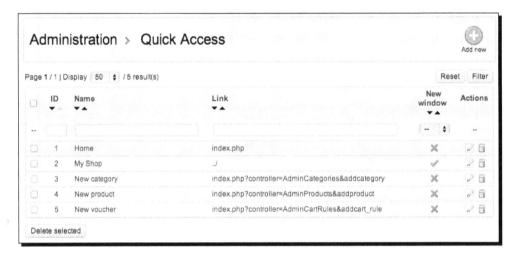

3. For the **Name** value, type Database backup.

4. For the **URL** value, type index.php?controller=AdminBackup.

5. Save your changes and try out your new quick access.

If you are looking to make your own quick accesses, then you are probably wondering how to get the value for the **URL** field. Go to the tab you are making the quick access and copy the URL on your browser. Then delete everything before index.php and everything from &token. I have copied the following database backup URL and highlighted the parts to delete so that you can see exactly what to delete and what to use:

```
http:/shop.com/adminpassword123456/index.php?controller=AdminBacku
p&token=37a0e13f7
```

## What just happened?

We made a quick access shortcut to the database backup feature. You can make quick access shortcuts to anything that is useful to you. The database backup feature is something that should be used regularly and we will discuss it in *Chapter 6, Security and Disaster Recovery*.

Let's see how much you have learned, remembered, and what you can work out by yourself.

## Pop quiz – tools and preferences challenge

Here are a number of questions about what you can do on the **Advanced Parameters**, **Administration**, and **Preferences** tabs. Just to make things more interesting, there are questions that deal with the previous chapters as well as this one.

Q1. How would you configure PrestaShop e-mail messages to be sent from your personal ISP account when you are running PrestaShop on your own PC?

1. It is not possible.

2. With an external SMTP server.

3. By selecting **Use PHP mail() function. Recommended; works in most cases**.

4. With a local SMTP server.

Q2. How can you reorder the main tabs?

1. By dragging-and-dropping them

2. By clicking on **Menus** under the **Administration** tab

3. By clicking on **General** under the **Preferences** tab

4. By clicking on **SEO & URLs** under the Preferences tab

Q3. We looked briefly at the database backup feature. Is backing up the database enough to ensure that you have everything you need to recover from a disaster?

1. Yes, PrestaShop does everything for us

2. Yes, but PrestaShop does a back up only for one table

3. No, PrestaShop has no right to run these kind of commands

4. No, but there is a module to do it

# E-mail marketing with newsletters

We will discuss marketing in *Chapter 8*, *Ready to Sell* and *Chapter 9*, *Go… To the Future*. However, newsletters, or e-mail marketing, is a special case. That is why it is worth discussing it here before we cover other marketing optionsin PrestaShop.

E-mail marketing is not just another type of marketing. In my opinion, it is absolutely crucial to maximize the potential of any online business. E-mail marketing with newsletters is a kind of catchall to make all other forms of marketing worthwhile. What do I mean by this?

E-mail marketing can support every other type of marketing you are doing. Think about all the different sources your website will eventually receive its visitors from – search engines due to your SEO efforts, paid adverts, link building, and social media marketing. If any of those phrases are alien to you, don't worry. They are all dealt with in *Chapter 8*, *Ready to Sell* and *Chapter 9*, *Go... To the Future*. The point to grasp here is that all the other methods when used on their own are actually prone to failure.

# Most people don't buy!

It's true. A vast majority of visits to your shop do not generate a sale. If you manage to achieve 10 percent your visits, you have done incredibly well. There are chances that the actual figure is nearer to 5 percent or lower. If we were working in a retail shop and 19 out of 20 customers we spoke to walked out with nothing, then we probably wouldn't last long before we had to find another job.

So this means we are expecting to fail 95 percent of the time. Now assuming that you have written a great sales copy, also provided compelling informational content, and have set up your PrestaShop correctly and smartly, there is still a little more you can do on your website itself. And it is probably not the fault of your website that 95 percent of your visitors kept their wallets firmly in their pockets.

## Why?

So why do 95 percent of your visitors leave without spending? There are lots of reasons—they aren't ready to buy, they want to do more research or they are looking to find a better price or service, and there are many more reasons as well. And what makes things worse is that when the customers have put things right in their minds and they finally have their wallet out, they are unlikely to remember your website. So we have to, as much as possible, remove this element of chance.

What if you could constantly remind your future potential customer? What if you could help them arrive at a buying decision? What if you could improve your relationship and warm up your potential customers with interesting and relevant industry or product information? You guessed it right, that's where e-mail marketing comes in. All the other forms of marketing bring people to your site—a small percentage will buy and e-mail marketing takes care of the rest.

Of course, you have to get the e-mail addresses of all these people and their permission to be contacted. And when you send e-mails, they must contain high quality compelling content to sell them your products.

## The stages of e-mail marketing

First we will look at how to start building a list of potential customers with the PrestaShop newsletter module. Then we will look at different ways to build that list as quickly as possible, and also capturing a high percentage of visitors. Then we will look at actually sending product notifications through PrestaShop alerts. Next we will look at a range of methods—PrestaShop and some more—for actually managing your list of names and your e-mail campaigns.

## Setting up the newsletter module

This is how we will begin to collect the e-mail addresses of willing subscribers. This brief tutorial creates a simple form for customers to enter their details and start receiving your e-mails. Like most things in PrestaShop, this is also a breeze. Follow the quick tutorial below.

## Time for action – the newsletter module

A couple of clicks is all it takes:

1. Click on the **Modules** tab, scroll down to the **Newsletter block**, installed by default. Be careful to configure the **Newsletter block** located in the **Front Office Features** category and not **Newsletter** in the **Analytics & Stats or Administration** category. We will look at the latter when we start sending e-mails/newsletters.

2. Scroll back down and click on **Configure**. Select the box for sending a confirmation. Then your new subscriber will get a very brief message confirming they have subscribed.

## *What just happened?*

Go and have a look at the newsletter subscription block that your customers will see:

Now we can go on to explore other e-mail communication topics.

# Switching on product notifications

Product notifications are different than newsletters but are a related topic. Switching on product notifications gives customers the option of receiving e-mails when out-of-stock products come back into stock. This works for actual customers who specifically request it, not newsletter subscribers, so it is still worth including new products and specials in your newsletters. We will talk more about newsletters in a minute. Now let's turn on product notifications.

## Time for action – product notifications

Here is how to do it.

1. Click on the **Modules** tab, scroll down to **Mail alerts** and install it.

2. Scroll back down to the module and click on **Configure**.

3. Make sure all of the boxes are checked.

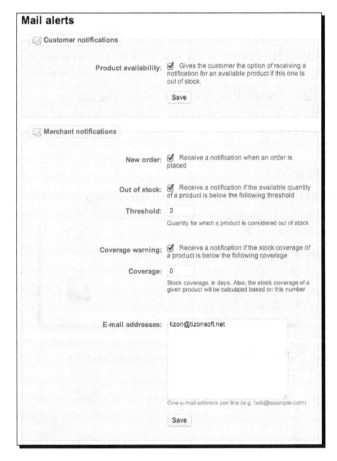

## *What just happened?*

You just provided a useful service for your customers.

Now back to e-mail marketing and newsletters for real. We will look at how to get lots of subscribers, create great e-mails, and then the different options available to send them. Another cool way to make your customers remember your shop is to allow them to configure their own reminder events Also, remember to tick the field **New order**, to receive a notification when an order is placed.

## Powerful newsletter modules

Newsletters are a good way to keep in touch with your customers because it is quite important to do so.

I recommend Mailchimp for Prestashop module. If you do not know about Mailchimp, it is a professional newsletter service with a different range of price, starting for free. You can download it for free from their official website at `http://connect.mailchimp.com/integrations/mailchimp-module-for-prestashop-free`

## Building a big list of subscribers

Now that your subscription block is ready to roll, let's look at a few ways of getting more subscribers from our visitors.

## Understanding what a newsletter is

Before sending newsletters to your subscribers you need to understand what is a newsletter, because it can cause a negative impact on your subscribers. Try not bothering your subscribers because your e-mails could be category for a spam. If your newsletters focus on your shop and offer something else, such as discounts, new products, then it will be welcomed by most subscribers.

### Incentives

Offer something for free if they sign up to your newsletter. Mention the free gift in your articles and the home page or other prominent pages. Here are some ideas for what to give away.

### What to give away

Think hard about your products, business, and industry. What would be really useful? If you are selling an information, music, or video product, it's easy. Perhaps offer a sample chapter, song, application, or video. If not that, why not create a downloadable PDF or a short video made on a webcam capturing the most compelling and useful information related to your products, business, or industry?

Here is another idea that might work for almost any business. Offer a free software download. Even if your website is not software related, you can always find great softwares that you can give away which has some connection with your industry. Visit www.sourceforge.net and find something suitable for your business.

If you're really stuck with incentives, offer a discount voucher. Consider very carefully before doing it because it needs to be viable financially. But what could be better way of making someone revisit your store?

## Offering more via e-mail

Write a really great article. You can then offer it as a reward for signing up. The other way (though a bit sneaky, it does work)—write another cool article but only publish part of it. Then offer the conclusion or vital final bit of information when they subscribe.

Okay, let's assume we will have hordes of subscribers. We now need to make some newsletters worth receiving.

# Creating newsletters

As with all your articles, you need to write interesting content that people actually want to read. The same rules apply for writing a great article for your website, but a newsletter needs more than just an article. You could use one or more of the following.

## Product information

This is just what it says. The very best buys, newest additions, or hottest products from your industry.

## Genuine news

Tell your readers about significant developments in the world of your niche. The hundredth annual teddy bear's picnic, or whatever is important to your visitors.

## Designing your newsletters

You are probably beginning to see that this topic is getting quite deep and there are lots of possibilities that can't be discussed here. How about this?

If your shop covers a relatively unchanging niche, such as teddy bears, then you probably know enough to get going. Write a new article following all the guidelines from *Chapter 4, Getting More Customers*. Put your company logo at the top and a special offer or two at the bottom and read on about how to send them. Mailchimp has a thousands of templates that you can modify according to your company for free.

If, on the other hand, your niche is a dynamic one with enthusiasts or lots of opinions, then this is where you can really capitalize on a great newsletter. You can send multiple newsletters with a different focus on the main types and format, and arrange them in many different ways to entice customers and maintain your readership. If this describes your niche, then it is worth putting a bit more effort and thought into the design, content, and type of your newsletter.

Now you have an idea of how to create a great e-mail newsletter. But how are you going to send it?

# Sending newsletters

Of course, once you have created interesting content and formatted it beautifully, you need to send it. Here are a number of ways you can do this—some free and some requiring the dreaded wallet.

## A quick word about spam

This is a complicated issue and varies greatly from country to country and in the US from state to state. In some places, you can do what you like, while in others, you could end up in jail for breaking one of the numerous communication or data protection laws. Here are a few rules:

- Never buy or borrow a list of e-mail addresses unless you are 100 percent certain that they have been gathered legitimately and all the recipients have signed up for e-mails from third parties (that is, you)
- Never add someone to your newsletter without their specific request
- Never use a person's e-mail after they have unsubscribed, no matter how much you think they might want to receive just one more
- Always include instructions to unsubscribe in every email

You need to be wary that even if you comply with all the laws and my guidelines mentioned above, where spam is concerned, the customer's perception is an important one. If a recipient thinks that the e-mail you have sent is a trash or doesn't identify it with the company he had signed up with, even if he had subscribed, he might click the **Mark as spam** button.

If this happens too often, then their ISP could mark your domain as spam. If you keep your content good and not too commercial as well as have a clear and easy unsubscribe process, then you should be able to avoid this.

## Using a PrestaShop module to send newsletters

As you might expect, there is a PrestaShop module for sending e-mails to your subscribers direct from your PrestaShop admin area. This is a quick download and is as easy to install as any other PrestaShop module.

As you know by now though, I don't like spending money! This module costs $64.80. If you want utter simplicity and $64.80 is not important to you, then you can go and buy the module from www.prestaworks.com.

If, like me, you don't want to get your wallet out, then read on. There are a number of ways to do it for free as well as point you in the direction of some pay-for services that can add extra frills to you newsletter campaigns. And because of the excellent PrestaShop facility to export a list of your subscribers, it is almost as easy as doing it through the PrestaShop module.

## Using your web host to send newsletters

Most web hosts offer an e-mail marketing package or a script that you can add to your site. I have never seen one that is both adequate and free (included with web hosting). Most either lack features or come with significant costs per month. However, have a look before you get your wallet out.

## A dedicated e-mail service provider to send newsletters

You can take up a new service with companies like Aweber (www.aweber.com) and MailChimp (www.mailchimp.com), and get a very easy-to-use and fully-featured service.

The big downside with these companies is that as your list grows, so does your expenses. Go and have a look at what these companies offer, but think carefully before getting your wallet out.

## A free e-mail system to send newsletters

Just what the doctor ordered! There is one that is fully-featured, fully–supported, and free. **phpList** is one of the several but is probably the best open source e-mail list management software system.

You can install it on your web host and then work through all the phases of starting and running an e-mail marketing campaign using phpList. It can help you build a list, create professional newsletters/e-mails, send them, manage replies, and give you statistical feedback.

phpList is very extensive and therefore cannot be explained fully in a few paragraphs here, but if you have decided that your e-mail/newsletter campaign is going to be an important part of your marketing strategy without paying extra money, this can be your solution.

## Getting your subscriber list

Whichever option you choose, you will need your list of subscribers. Here is how to get the list in a text file so that you can copy and paste them into your preferred sending method.

# Time for action – accessing your e-mail list

We will use the PrestaShop admin area to create a .CSV file that can be used to copy and paste all your subscribers into your preferred system.

1. Click on the **Modules** tab and scroll down to the **Newsletter** module and click on **Install**. This module is in the **Administration** category.

2. Now click on **Configure**.

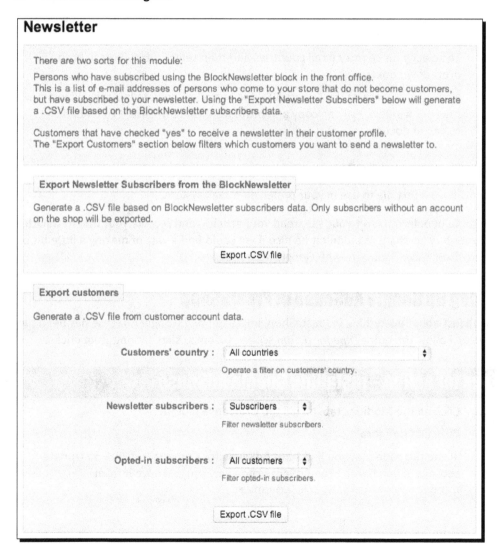

3.  You have two buttons where you can click to export a `.CSV` file.

4.  The first will export a list of everybody who signed up using your newsletter signup block.

5.  The second exports a list of everyone who has created a customer account. Notice here that you have some options for filtering/customizing the second list. You have the option to select a specific country or all countries. You also have the option to choose subscribers or non-subscribers from opted-in customers and newsletter subscribers. This is important. Never send newsletters to anybody who has not subscribed. You will get a bad reputation, end up on ISP block lists, and in some parts of the world you might even be prosecuted.

6.  So select your country or all countries and then select subscribers in both drop-down boxes.

7.  Now click on each of the **Export .CSV file** buttons. The data is displayed in a new browser window. You can copy and paste from there or save it to a Windows Notepad document.

## What just happened?

You now have a text file to use in your preferred e-mail system.

Now some people who visit your site, read your articles, and receive your free newsletter will never buy anything. Wouldn't it be nice if we could find a way of making a little bit of revenue from them? You can, with Google AdSense.

## Setting up Google AdSense in PrestaShop

As with just about everything in PrestaShop, implementing Google AdSense has been nice and easy. Follow the quick *Time for action* section below to start earning from clicks.

## Time for action – installing Google AdSense

1.  Click on the **Modules** tab. Install the **GAdsense** module.

2.  Click on **Configure**.

3.  Paste the code that you had from **AdSense for Content** and click on **Update settings**. If you haven't the AdSense code yet, you can have it from `https://www.google.com/adsense`.

4. Wait for half an hour and visit your shop front to see the advert.

## What just happened?

Your adverts will start running fairly soon. A quick word of warning, just in case you didn't read Google's terms and conditions. One key thing to remember is that you must never ever click on your own adverts. Google will pick up on this and will not give you many chances before it does something really annoying.

# Setting up PrestaShop statistics

Now you are up and running (or at least you're in the starting blocks) and it is a good time to consider a way to measure the success of your site. If you can't take measurements, you won't know whether the things you're doing is right or wrong. This and the next section will introduce two schemes for achieving this. First, as the heading suggests, is **PrestaShop statistics**.

PrestaShop statistics, in my opinion, are unrivalled in free software. The depth of information and richness of presentation are literally second to none. As if this were not enough, PrestaShop statistics is an absolute breeze to set up.

# Graph and grid engines

These are the parts of PrestaShop that power the presentation of the statistics. Depending upon which engine you choose, the graph or chart you are using will be presented a bit differently. Or you could switch them all off and just view the basic manner in which PrestaShop presents things.

One way I suggest is to switch all of them on because you can flip between the different engines while viewing statistics and then decide what you like best. Then you can turn off the ones that are unnecessary. We will do this in a *Time for action* section shortly.

# Statistics modules

These are the different modules that present and collect statistics that you can use to find interesting or useful information about your store. As with engines, a good way of exploring these is to switch them all on, and then go to explore them. We will do this in the next *Time for action*. However, we will not go too deeply into how you can actually use them until we look at analyzing statistics in *Chapter 9, Go… To the Future*. For now we will just familiarize ourselves with what is available.

So let's do it.

# Time for action – setting up statistics engines and modules

As I mentioned earlier, we will switch everything on:

1. Click on the **Modules** tab. Scroll down to the **Analytics and Stats** section and install the first one. Repeat this until they are all installed. There is no configuration required for any of these. By default PrestaShop has the most important ones installed.

2. Click on the **Home** option in the **Quick Access** drop-down list. Now you have a quick statistical summary on your admin home page.

3. Now click on the **Stats** tab. Notice that there are lot of things to explore. This is what we will do now.

# What just happened?

Now your website will begin to gather statistics and you can then make meaningful decisions based on what they tell you.

# Exploring the statistics options

Let's have a brief explanation of the main options that appear on the **Stats** tab; if your store has no customers yet, then you won't be able to see much:

| | |
|---|---|
| **Visits and Visitors** | Helps you to know how many returning visitors you have by comparing the number of visits by unique visitors. |
| **Sales and orders** | Gives a lot of sales information. |
| **Customer accounts** | This is useful stuff. It tells you how many registered customers are there from a particular time period. It also tell you how many customers gave up during registration or registered, but decided not to buy. |
| **Registered Customer Info** | This option will give you some useful customer demographics. These include age, sex, country, and currency. |
| **Visitors online** | This helps to see if there are people browsing your shop, what they are looking at, and most importantly, whether they have something in their cart. This module can distinguish between a regular visitor and a logged-in customer. |
| **Best vouchers** | This tells you about the vouchers you have created and how well they do. We will cover more on vouchers in *Chapter 8, Ready to Sell*. |
| **Best customers** | Tells you which customers spent the most. |
| **Visitors origin** | Tells you which search engines and websites sent visitors to you. |
| **Pages not found** | This lists URLs that people have attempted to access but were not found. This is useful for finding potential linking problems. |
| **Search engine keywords** | Find out which keywords brought traffic to your site. |
| **Product details** | This gives you a quick summary of products and stock levels. |
| **Best products** | This option provides a league table of best-selling products. |
| **Best categories** | Just as it says—it lists the categories that do the best in your shop. |
| **Best suppliers** | Says which suppliers supply the best-selling products. |

| | |
|---|---|
| **Carrier distribution** | A detailed look at the different carrier services your customers choose. |
| **Shop search** | This provides a league table of search terms used in your shop and how often they have been used. This can be really useful for picking new aliases and other things as well. |

# Installing Google Analytics

It has to be said that Google Analytics is really quite impressive. If you want to know (and as a switched-on web master, you would want to know) who visited your site, where they live, what operating system and browser they have, what pages they visited, how long they stayed, where they got the link to your site from, what websites are sending you visitors, and much more, then Google Analytics is for you! And what does it cost? Absolutely nothing!

## Getting a Google Analytics account

Go to `http://www.google.com/analytics/` and click on **Sign Up Now**. Follow the simple instructions to open an Analytics account.

The budding e-commerce entrepreneur is often left trawling forums with contradictory comments or advice based on an old version of Analytics. And then there was PrestaShop.

## Have a go hero – doing more with the thing

Have a go at this. Make sure that you have signed up for Google Analytics already and then have a go at this challenge. Also make sure that you are logged into PrestaShop and your Analytics account. Now hold your breath. Can you install Google Analytics in PrestaShop without breathing? [Only joking! Please do not try this at home! We take no responsibility for the consequences if you actually do this.]

## Time for action – installing Google Analytics

Just perform the following steps and ignore Google's additional warnings and instructions because PrestaShop is different. Go!

1. In your Analytics account, click on **Add Website Profile** and type in your domain name.

2. Note the **Web Property ID** in the **Tracking Status Information** box.

**3.** In PrestaShop, click on the **Modules** tab. Scroll to the **Analytics and Stats** category and install the **ganalytics** module.

**4.** Scroll back down to the **Google Analytics** module and click on **Configure**.

**5.** Enter your **Analytics Web Property ID** in the box and click on **Save**.

**6.** Breathe.

**7.** If this is not your book and your partner has a blue face and their head on their keyboard, please call an ambulance. Please note the publisher and the author accepts no responsibility for death or serious injury while reading this book.

## What just happened?

Tracking has now been installed. Data will be gathered and you would have meaningful statistics in around 24 hours. We will cover much more on statistics in *Chapter 9, Go… To the Future*.

## Using Google Analytics

Just log in to your Analytics account and have a look. Click on some of the options and suboptions in the main menu on the left-hand side. There won't be any data there yet, but as you can see there is an abundance of possibilities. In *Chapter 9, Go… To the Future*, we will discuss in detail a plan to make your PrestaShop a roaring success, with Google Analytics playing a big part in it.

# Summary

We learned a lot in this chapter. It was probably the most diverse chapter. A sort of mopping up, if you like, to make sure we appreciate the diversity PrestaShop has to offer before we move on.

Specifically, we covered the following topics:

- We now have a very good knowledge of the **Preferences** tab.
- The **Advanced Parameters** and **Administration** tabs have been explored.
- We have a good understanding of e-mail/newsletter campaigns and our different options for implementing them.
- We have a range of powerful tools for analyzing statistics. We also looked at the range of data available but put off actually analyzing anything until *Chapter 9, Go... To the Future.*

Now how would you feel if after all this work your web host had a catastrophe and you lost the lot? That really would be a bad day! So without any delay we will move on to the next chapter and look at security, backing up your store, and recovering from a disaster.

# 6
# Security and Disaster Recovery

*In this chapter, we will do everything possible to make sure that our store does not become the victim of a successful attack. Fortunately, the PrestaShop team takes security very seriously and issues updates and fixes as soon as any problems are discovered.*

*We just have to make sure we do everything we can and implement the PrestaShop upgrades as soon as they are available. All this is covered in this chapter.*

*It is also vital for us to always have a recent copy of our store because one day our shop might die on us; it is probably inevitable. It might be a hacker, or we might accidentally muck it up ourselves. A recent backup to handle this type of event is a minor inconvenience, because without one, it could be an expensive catastrophe.*

In this chapter, we shall:

- ◆ Look at ways in which your shop can be damaged
- ◆ Add users, profiles, and permissions to increase security
- ◆ Talk about and optionally implement SSL to protect your customers' private information
- ◆ Learn how to back up and restore your shop in case everything else fails
- ◆ Talk about upgrading PrestaShop and how this helps in keeping your business secure

So let's get on with it...

# Types of attacks

There are different types of security attacks. Here is a very brief explanation of some of the most common ones. Hopefully, this will help to clarify why security is an ongoing and evolving issue and not something that can ever be 100 percent solved out-of-the-box.

## Common sense issues

These are often overlooked. Make sure your passwords are impossible to guess; use number sequences that are memorizable to you but unimaginable and meaningless to everyone else. Combine number sequences with a variety of upper and lower case letters. Don't share your passwords with anyone. This applies to anyone who has access to your shop or hosting account.

## Brute force

This is when an attacker uses software to repeatedly attempt to gain access to or discover a password by guessing. Clearly, the simplest defense against this is a secure password. A good password is one with upper and lower case characters, apparently random numbers, and words that are not names or can be found in the dictionary. Does your administrator password stand up to these criteria?

## SQL injection attack

A malicious person can amend, delete, or retrieve information from your database by cleverly manipulating the forms or database requests contained in PrestaShop code. By appending this to legitimate PrestaShop database code, harm can be done or breaches of security can be achieved.

## Cross-site scripting

Attackers add instructions to access code on another site. They do this by appending a URL (pointing to malicious code) to a PHP URL of a legitimate page on your site.

## User error

This is straight forward. It is likely that while developing or amending your website, you will mess up some or perhaps all of your PrestaShop store. I did it once while writing this chapter. I will give you the full details of my experiment and my slightly embarrassing confession later.

So with so many ways that things can go wrong, we better start looking at some solutions.

# Employees and user security

If you plan to employ someone, or if you have a partner who is going to help with your new shop, it makes good sense to create a new user account so that they have their own login details. Even if it will be only you who needs to use the PrestaShop control panel, there is still a good argument for creating two or more accounts. Here's why.

First we will consider a scenario, though a slightly exaggerated one:

◆ Bikes4U.com

Bikes4U wants to offer articles about how to use its products. The management, probably correctly, believe that in-depth how-tos about all its products will boost sales and increase customer retention.

The diverse nature of their products makes employing a single writer impossible. For example, an expert on mountain bikes will rarely be an expert on unicycles. And a user of folding bikes probably won't know about clipless pedals.

This is quite a problem. The management decides they need a way to allow a whole team of freelance writers who can login directly to the PrestaShop CMS. But bearing in mind the highly dubious backgrounds some of these writers will have, how can they be trusted in the PrestaShop control panel?

◆ Users of Bikes4U.com

Suppose you employ somebody to write articles for you. You don't really want them to be able to play with product prices or payment modules. You would want to restrict them to the CMS area of the control panel. Similarly, your partner might be helping you wrap and pack your products. To avoid accidents, you might like to restrict them to the **Customers** and **Orders** tab.

Now consider this scenario. Even you, after reading this book, could make a mistake. It is a really good idea to create at least one extra user account for yourself. I always make myself a wrapping and packing account. I use it all the time, and it is reassuring to know that I can't accidentally click on anything that can cause a problem.

This type of user security is common in large organizations. On a company intranet, employees will almost always be restricted to areas of the company system which they need, and nothing more.

The following *Time for action* section shows you how to create a new user account; after that, we will look at profiles and permissions to enforce the restrictions suitable to us.

Okay, now let's create a new user.

# Time for action – creating users

As you have come to expect, this is really easy.

**1.** Hover over the **Administration** tab, click on **Employees**, and then click on the **Add new** button.

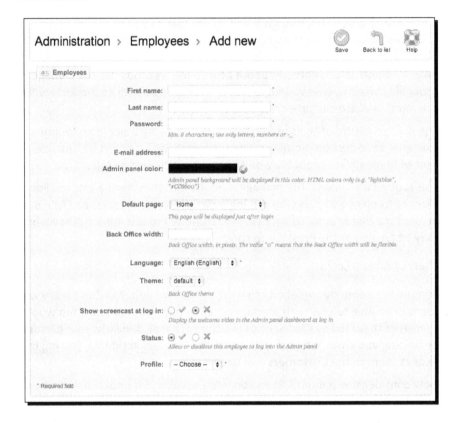

**2.** Enter the information of your new employee or user in the required fields.

**3.** The **Status** box enables you to allow or disallow access to the new employee. Unless you have a reason for creating an account for an employee and not letting them use it, select the radio button for the green check mark. If you have reason to want to stop your new employee or user from accessing your control panel, simply come back to this page and select the red cross mark.

**4.** In the **Profile** drop-down box, choose **Administrator** to give the new user full access. We will investigate when this is a good idea and when you might like to change it; for example, if you're adding a freelance writer next.

**5.** Click on the **Save** button to create the new user account.

## *What just happened?*

The new user can now log in to the control panel and perform any task.

# Profiles

This section on profiles and the next topic, *Permissions*, are very closely linked to users. A profile is like a position. You can create a profile and assign responsibilities and restrictions. The administrator profile created by default can do everything in the control panel. As we discussed previously, this might not be the ideal situation for you.

What we will do now is create a new profile called "customer service". In the next section on permissions, we will assign the appropriate permissions to this new profile. Allowing all users with the customer service profile to access everything they need to do their job and restricting their access to anything that is not part of their job, significantly reduces the possibility of accidents or, dare I say it, malicious actions, by a disgruntled employee or someone who gains access to their account.

## Time for action – creating profiles

We will now create a profile in a couple of steps:

1. Hover over the **Administration** tab and click on **Profiles**, and subsequently click on the green **Add new** button.

2. Type in Customer Service or whatever you want your first profile to be called.

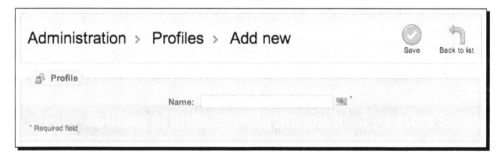

3. Click on **Save**. Now read on about permissions.

## *What just happened?*

We have just created a user profile to which we can assign users. But to make the profile meaningful and worthwhile, we will now assign appropriate permissions to it, which are explained in the next section.

# Permissions

In the *Time for action* section that follows, we will assign the permissions that are appropriate for an employee with customer service and packing responsibilities. First we will take a look at the options in general, for permissions.

## Permissions and their levels

There are four types of permissions: **View**, **Add**, **Edit**, and **Delete**. PrestaShop controls access by allowing you to assign these types of permissions to any of the tabs and subtabs.

You can restrict the members of a profile from viewing any tab(s) you like. For example, you might not want the customer service profile to change anything on the **Payment** tab. No problem; you can totally remove this tab for the users of that profile. In the Bikes4U freelance writer scenario, you may want to create users who only have access to the **CMS** tab. You could do this by removing, or as we will see in a bit, not adding any permissions apart from the ones for the **CMS** tab.

So to stop the users of a particular profile from adding and removing products, you need to remove the **Add** and **Delete** permissions from the **Catalog** tab. These users would then be able to edit product descriptions, but they will not be able to add or remove products by themselves.

The depth of information we have just discussed is almost certainly adequate for any new shop, and also if you are an existing business owner and you intend to hand over the running of your PrestaShop store to your staff. The key with permissions, profiles, and users is planning. Take time to consider your company structure, which users should have access to what, and create a profile for each. Once that is done, read on to configure permissions for those profiles.

Now that we have looked at the different permissions, you will easily be able to decide which ones are the most appropriate for the different profiles you want to make for your shop.

## Time for action – configuring permissions to profiles

Of course, the permissions and levels that I've suggested in this *Time for action* section are just my views. You will know best as to what is most appropriate for your business. Let's get on with it then.

1. Hover over the **Administration** tab, click on **Permissions**, and select the **Customer Service** profile, or whatever profile you are configuring from the left-hand side menu.

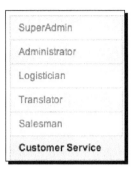

**2.** Take time to examine the tabs and the options associated with them.

**3.** Try adding permissions for one of the tabs. For the freelance writer, I would just enable the **View** functionality for the **Tools** tab and the **View**, **Add**, and **Edit** functionalities for the **CMS** tab. The reason we need to assign **View** to **Tools** is because the **CMS** tab will not be visible otherwise.

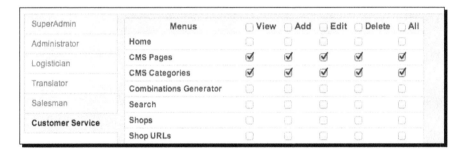

**4.** Go back to a user's subtab in **Employees**, edit the user, and assign the profile you have just amended to the user. Now log in as that user and see the changes taking effect.

**5.** Now log in again as the administrator and make the rest of the changes you decided upon.

## What just happened?

You have now created your first profile. It should be simple to create as many profiles as you like. Also, don't forget to assign your users to profiles appropriate for them.

## Pop quiz – security

Q1. Can you think of a good reason as to why you need to assign permissions to profiles and then profiles to users, instead of assigning permissions directly to users?

1. In order to be consistent with every profile.

2. Because PrestaShop can't handle another way.

3. Because there aren't any particular reasons for doing it in this way.

4. Because other e-commerce software do it in the same way.

Q2. Taking into account the different types of attacks and other things that can go wrong, what do users, profiles, and permissions protect against?

1. The deletion of items.

2. The deletion of items and changes in the design of our store.

3. The changes in the design of our store, addition or deletion of another employee, and modification of orders, among others.

4. They do not protect our store against anything.

Q3. How can we protect users' login information from being sniffed out by people listening for information?

1. Using SSL.

2. Using FTP.

3. Using SMTP.

4. Using WWW.

# SSL – Secure Sockets Layer

SSL is a cool system or, in tech speak, a protocol for allowing encrypted communication over the Internet. The need for this is obvious when you think about the type of information that must be given and received, even for the simplest transaction. A customer's personal details and credit card details are the most obvious examples of these types of information.

By encrypting (making information incomprehensible to all but the intended recipient), you can take your customers' money and personal details without worrying that their private details will be intercepted by a third party.

Regular encryption relies on the sharing of a decryption key. A decryption key, simply speaking, is a mathematical formula for making the incomprehensible information comprehensible again. SSL uses a method known as public key cryptography that allows a website, such as yours, to give an encryption key to your customer's web browser, which encrypts the confidential information before sending it. The SSL web server has a private key known only to itself, which can descramble the information and retrieve your customer's confidential information.

# Shared SSL, dedicated SSL, or no SSL

Shared SSL is usually free. Dedicated SSL, on the other hand, will certainly cost you a few dollars per month.

Almost any web server can be configured to be an SSL server. In most hosting environments, you will be offered a shared SSL server for free. This is where you have your communications re-routed through an SSL-enabled server. The problem is that the SSL server has a different address from the server that your website is actually hosted on. PrestaShop has not been designed to be able to easily use a shared SSL server.

If, however, you must have SSL and absolutely do not want to get your wallet out to pay for a dedicated SSL certificate, then have a read of this article on the PrestaShop forums: `http://www.prestashop.com/forums/viewthread/19232/`.

Do not despair! If you want or need SSL without the technical hassles, then you will need to contact your web host and arrange to buy a dedicated SSL certificate for your website. You shouldn't need to do anything technical. Just pay, wait for it to be set up, and then follow the easy tutorial explained next. PrestaShop will then use `https://` instead of `http://` as the protocol for any relevant page on your website, and your customers will be protected.

So SSL sounds like a good idea. But it is not an absolute must. If you are using PayPal to take payments, then all your customers' financial details will be dealt with on the PayPal website anyway. And they use their own SSL server, as you would expect. Consider that the name and address of your customers is entered on your website. Is this a security problem? Will your customers object to their names and addresses being retrieved unencrypted? Only you can decide.

Another potential drawback of not using SSL is that your login information to the control panel will be left unencrypted. Do you use wireless Internet? Perhaps in a busy location with lots of other wireless users, it is possible for somebody to obtain your username and password. Then they can do whatever they like with it.

The other consideration with SSL is that more and more customers look for the `https://` prefix in the address bar when going through checkout. And most web browsers display a nice graphical padlock and maybe some other reassuring embellishments like green address bars. So even if in your opinion you don't *need* SSL, it might be worthwhile even if it is just for show.

So decide whether you want shared or dedicated SSL, or none at all. Read the next tutorial after setting up SSL with your web host, if you are going to use it.

## Setting up SSL in PrestaShop

This is so easy. Many shopping carts require editing of the PHP code in multiple files, even for dedicated SSL. Again, well done PrestaShop! Perhaps you can make shared SSL easy in a future revision as well.

## Time for action – setting up SSL in PrestaShop

Let's do it.

1. Hover over the **Preferences** tab and click on **General**.
2. For the first item in the list of options (**Enable SSL**), select **Yes**.
3. Scroll to the bottom of the page and click on **Save**.
4. Now go to your shop front, log in to your account, and notice the **https://** at the front of the web address in your browser.

### *What just happened?*

Your customers' vital details are now encrypted by SSL. If you are going to use PayPal as your payment provider, then the customers' financial details are kept secure by PayPal, even if you opted not to use SSL on your website.

## Making a copy of your store

We have taken a number of steps to protect your PrestaShop store, but what if it all goes wrong anyway? It is still possible, although much less likely, that your site will get hacked. It is also possible that we might accidentally spoil our own PrestaShop store. If you promise not to tell anyone else, I will give you an example of a self-inflicted disaster I had.

While working on this chapter, I was playing with the **Permissions** features. I deleted a few tabs and then with a single inadvertent click, I deleted the **Employees** tab! The permissions page went blank and there was no way to restore all the tabs that I had deleted. I can't put in print what I said when I realized my mistake.

But I had a copy and the page was up and running again in 10 minutes.

A lesson to be taken from this incident is to create a new profile and user for you. Call it *Junior admin*, and then if you do something dumb like I did, you can log in as the administrator and make it right.

So our objective for this section is to create an offline, untouchable, and easily usable backup. Then no matter what happens, you will be able to get your business up and running in around 10 minutes. And no matter how talented and resourceful a hacker is, I guarantee that he or she won't be able to get remote access to a CD stored in your locked cupboard!

# Introducing the backup process

Two main areas will be covered in these step-by-step tutorials. Coming up next, we will back up the PrestaShop database. The database is separate from the files in your web space on your web host. It holds information that is accessed by the code contained in the PrestaShop files.

The second part of the backup process is obtaining a full copy of the PrestaShop files. This is nice and simple, but we will still do it step by step to be 100 percent certain that we are never left with a problem that can't be fixed.

## Frequency

So how often should you make a backup? It all depends on the frequency of change to your store. Let's say you get ten purchasing customers a day. If you backup every week but suddenly get hacked just before you do a backup, you would lose the details of 70 customers and their orders. In most businesses, this would be quite a dire situation.

Now when you first open your PrestaShop site, you might not get an order for some weeks. So does this mean an infrequent backup would be okay? Maybe yes. But when your PrestaShop site is new, you are probably going to be making more regular configuration changes. Some or all of these could be lost if you don't have a recent backup.

Only you can answer the question of how often to do a complete backup. This will obviously depend upon the frequency of change to your PrestaShop files and database. I will show you how to take a backup that is fast and trouble-free, although there isn't really any reason not to do it daily. Obviously though, it is up to you.

# Backing up your database

PrestaShop has a handy database backup utility. This makes backing up your store a breeze. Here's how to do it.

## Time for action – backing up your database

Log in to your PrestaShop control panel and read on.

1. Hover over the **Advanced Parameters** tab and click on **DB Backup**.
2. Read the disclaimer and click on **I have read the disclaimer - Create a new Backup**. Wow, that was quick! We are almost done.

3. Now click on the link that says **Download the Backup file**, and save the file to your hard disk. If the files on your web host are destroyed, your PrestaShop database takes the backup; unless you have downloaded the backup, it is destroyed with them. Always download each backup file after creation.

4. Click on **Back to list** and you will notice that PrestaShop keeps a nicely ordered list of the database backups you have made. Just be aware of the fact that PrestaShop doesn't keep a record of whether you have actually downloaded the backup file. So the previous step is really crucial.

## What just happened?

You now have a backup of your PrestaShop database. It shouldn't have taken more than a minute. We will look at how to use your database backup soon.

## Backing up your files

You probably already know how to do this, but as it is so crucial, we will go through it step by step.

## Time for action – backing up your files

We are going to use FTP, so have your web host's FTP username and password handy, and then read on.

1. Open an FTP window on your web space containing the PrestaShop files.

2. Open a second Explorer window in a folder where you want to keep your backup files. You can use a dedicated FTP application as mentioned before.

3. Highlight all the files on the web server and drag them to the **Backup** folder. It might take some time for the download to finish; obviously, you don't need to be there to watch it happen.

4. Sometimes, the download fails. It is very difficult to ascertain exactly at what point to resume the download; the safest policy when this happens is to start the whole download again. If the download fails on a regular basis, get into the habit of copying the folders one at a time. This does demand much more of your attention, but you can easily do something else between managing folders.

5. To be absolutely sure that your backup is safe, copy it to a CD, DVD, memory stick, external hard drive; wherever you like.

## What just happened?

You now have a complete, usable backup. With the one caveat of your FTP download probably failing, there is only a very tiny demand on your time even if you do this daily.

Now let's look at how to use your backup in the event of disaster.

# Using your copy

Using your backup is not too tricky, and because of the importance of the topic, we will go through it a step at a time.

## Restoring the database

To do this, we will need to get a little bit more technical than when we took a backup of your database. We will need to use a database tool called **PHPMyAdmin**, provided by our web hosts .

Many web hosts provide access to databases hosted with them through PHPMyAdmin; in the unlikely event that your web host doesn't, contact technical support and ask them for the equivalent of this tool. It should then be fairly simple to interpret the instructions given in the next *Time for action* section.

As every web host is different, I will mention shortcuts and some potential problems (along with their solutions) that are web host-dependent. What is fairly sure is that at some point you will need access to a web-based program provided by your web hosts, like PHPMyAdmin. Hence, we will look at that first.

## Time for action – how to restore the database

Log in to your web host's control panel. Find **PHPMyAdmin**. Among all of the hosts that are in use, it can be accessed by viewing the list of databases and then clicking on **Edit** or **Manage with PHPMyAdmin**. Then a screen very similar to the next screenshot is shown by clicking on the edit link next to the PrestaShop database. All the functions that we carry out in this tutorial will be performed on that specific database.

When you have located PHPMyAdmin or your web host's equivalent, read on.

1. Open a new browser window or tab. In your web host's control panel, delete the database.

2. Recreate the database using the same name, username, and password. A potential problem here is that some web hosts do not let you choose the name of a database. Don't panic, just create a new database and proceed with whatever name they give you. An extra step that I point out near the end of this tutorial should solve the problem.

3. Extract the compressed database backup on your hard disk so that you are left with a file named `something.sql`.

4. Go to your PHPMyAdmin control panel and click on **Databases**, and you will see the screen change to display a row of tabs across the top. They look like the ones in the following screenshot:

5. Click on the database for which you would like to import your backup, and click on the **Import** tab after that. Browse to your extracted database backup and select the file. You will also need to click on the **Go** button on the PHPMyAdmin page. A few seconds later, your database will be restored.

6. If you created a database with the same username and password, you can skip the rest of this tutorial. If not, you have a bit more to do.

7. Among your backup files, you need to open a file from the `config` folder using Notepad. The file is named `settings.inc.php`.

8. There, you will see a list of database configuration parameters. Simply copy and paste your new database name, server address, username and password to overwrite the old ones. Save the file and read on.

## What just happened?

You now have a perfectly restored database.

## Restoring the files

This is much simpler and quicker than restoring the database. Simply put, we need to replace all the files on the web server with the files from our backup.

## Time for action – restoring your files

1. Open an FTP connection to your web server.

2. Delete all the PrestaShop files on your web server.

3. Upload all the backup files. Be sure to upload them in the exact same structure in which they existed previously. For example, if you stored the backup files in a folder, don't upload the folder they were stored in as well.

4. As with backing up your files, if you get errors when dragging all the files and folders at once, retry doing the process using a folder or two at a time. Don't forget the "loose" files that reside in the main directory and not in any of the PrestaShop folders.

5. Visit your shop front and the PrestaShop control panel to see if they are working.

6. Breathe a sigh of relief.

## What just happened?

You have just deployed a backup of your store.

## Assessing what went wrong

The first thing to do is check whether you have the latest version of PrestaShop installed. Upgrading is covered in a minute. Other than that, the causes of a hack attack can be difficult to assess. Take a look at the upcoming *Have a go hero* section to learn and think about some extra precautions to prevent the recurrence of such an attack.

## Have a go hero – securing your newly restored shop

So what if the security problem arose because the hacker had your database username, address, or your admin password? How can you stop exactly the same thing from happening tomorrow? You can find the answer to these questions by following the steps given here:

1. Create a new database with a different name, username, and password through your web host's control panel.

2. Import the backup file for the new database just as you did for the original. Then in your PrestaShop folder, you need to open a file from the `config` folder using Notepad. The file is named `settings.inc.php.control`.

3. Now enter the details of your new database. Be sure to get them exactly the same. Click on **Save**. Your hacker must again start discovering the details of your database.

4. Now click on the **Employees** tab, click on the **Edit** icon and type in a new password. Click on **Save**.

5. If the hacker used your password, he now needs to start again.

# Upgrading PrestaShop

PrestaShop will add new features and enhancements from time to time. Of course, it is great to be able to add these improvements to your shop.

The main reason to keep your shop up-to-date at all times is because the updates include security fixes, that is, changes to PrestaShop that make it less likely and harder for a malicious person to mess up your hard work or compromise your customer's security.

## Time for action – how to upgrade PrestaShop

Keeping PrestaShop up-to-date will keep us secure against all the known threats. So let's do it.

1. Make sure you have a full backup of your store, files, and database in case this goes horribly wrong. And it can.

2. Log in to your PrestaShop control panel. If there is an update available, it will be shown near the top of your admin login page. If not, you could revisit this tutorial when there is one.

3. Click on the **Download** link and save the upgrade. Yours will probably have a different version number from the one in the screenshot.

4. Extract the download and you will be left with a `prestashop` folder full of subfolders and files.

5. Rename your main `prestashop` folder and leave it on your website. Call it `prestashop_old`. We are doing this so that in a few steps time, we would easily be able to copy back some files to the new folder. You can perform this step in your web host's control panel or by opening an FTP window, right-clicking the folder and selecting **Rename**, and then renaming it to `prestashop_old`.

6. Now recreate an empty folder with the same name as your original `prestashop` folder (the one you just renamed).

7. Upload all the files and folders within the `upgrade` folder to the folder where PrestaShop was located originally. You now have the latest versions of the PrestaShop files on your server. But what about all your configurations?

8. Copy the `/img` directory from your old folder to the folder with the upgraded files.

9. Copy the `/modules` directory from your old folder to the folder with the upgraded files.

**10.** If you have installed any new themes, copy the `/themes/newtheme` directory from your old folder to the folder with the upgraded files.

**11.** Compare the contents of the old and new `.htaccess` files in the main directory. Add any parts in the old file that are not present in the new file, to the new file. Don't simply copy them across folders because the upgrade might include some amendments. Simply copying the files across would remove these changes.

**12.** Copy your `sitemap.xml` file from the old files to the new ones.

**13.** Copy the `config/settings.inc.php` file from the old folder to the new one.

**14.** Run the installer and do things just as before, but select **update** on the first page. PrestaShop knows you are performing updates due to the presence of the `settings.inc.php` file. When you're ready, type in `www.yourshop.com/install`.

**15.** On the next page of the update wizard, you will see a warning. If you followed this guide, you have already done so. Click on the **I certify** button, and then click on the **Next** button.

**16.** When you're done, just as before, delete the `install` folder and rename the `admin` folder.

If you think that this is very complicated, PrestaShop now has a module to do an auto upgrade. The module's name is **1-click Upgrade**. You still need to remember to do a backup, because this module is experimental; my experience with it has been 99% positive.

Sometimes, when you do a major upgrade from Version 1.x to 1.y, you need to rewrite the theme. Again, please do a backup before you do this.

## What just happened?

You now have the latest version of PrestaShop up and running.

Okay, I admit it. That wasn't pretty. Upgrading PrestaShop is a little bit of a chore. This is one of the few areas where other shopping carts do a little better. But it's not so bad either. Half an hour's work every couple of months to get the latest features and security fixes shouldn't really be a huge problem.

Have a look at this quick challenge that is related to upgrading PrestaShop.

## Have a go hero – keeping your store live while upgrading

While all the various processes are going on, during an upgrade, your shop is offline. When brand new, this is probably not a problem. But what about in a year or two when you are serving hundreds of customers at a time? Being offline is obviously unacceptable!

How would you perform the upgrade without affecting your stores availability? (A clue is that it involves temporarily having two sets of working files using the same database.)

The answer is, simply perform the upgrade in a new folder; you could call it `prestashop_new`. Now you can copy across your settings as before but, this time, from a live folder. When you run the installer, don't forget to type in `www.yourshop.com/prestashop_new/install`. When you have finished, rename the original folder to `prestashop_old` and rename `prestashop_new` to the name of your original PrestaShop folder (pointed to by your domain name).

# This chapter in a nutshell

There is lots you can do to protect your PrestaShop site. But there is always a way in which a determined attacker can find a flaw with your security. Do everything you can; in fact, I suggest you read up further on general web security. A good starting point is an excellent article I found via the PrestaShop forums. Here it is:

`http://www.smashingmagazine.com/2010/01/14/web-security-primer-are-you-part-of-the-problem/`

But remember, you are never totally secure. Always have a very recent backup that is ready for use.

# Summary

We have learned a lot in this chapter about malicious attacks, user-caused problems, how to avoid them, and how to recover from them when all else fails.

Specifically, we covered the following topics:

- The most common types of malicious attacks and some problems that can be caused by legitimate users
- User security using groups and permissions
- SSL for our customers and our own privacy
- Keeping PrestaShop up-to-date and safe from known attacks by upgrading PrestaShop to the latest version
- Creating and using a backup

Now that we have this essential information under our belts, it is time to look at how we actually get money from our customers and the different ways in which this can be achieved with PrestaShop payment modules.

# 7
# Checkouts and Shipping

*In this chapter we will configure and set up anything and everything related to receiving payments. This will include the actual mechanism for getting customers' money from their account to yours, as well as a number of other important related topics.*

In this chapter, we shall:

- ◆ Choose and set up a payment provider
- ◆ Look at alternative payment methods
- ◆ Take a look at sales taxes
- ◆ Discuss and implement gift vouchers
- ◆ Learn how to accept foreign currencies
- ◆ Look at the multitude of different ways to set up shipping options for your customers to choose from and make sure they get charged correctly

Here we go then...

## Handling payments

There are a number of interrelated issues with regard to payment handling, some of which are not obviously apparent. This is one of those times where I recommend to read about payment providers and currencies, to completely understand the best option that fits your business.

# Which payment provider should I use?

This is an interesting question. The three big players that we will cover specifically are Google Checkout, PayPal and Amazon payments. There are a few comparisons between them that should help you choose the best option for you. First, a few words about merchant accounts.

## Merchant accounts

A merchant account is where you use a company, sometimes called a "gateway", to handle the actual transaction, but the customer's payment is deposited directly into your account. This sounds great and in some ways it is, but it's not always a good option. Another advantage is that you are probably less prone to being defrauded by a customer. This is because regular credit card chargeback rules apply. Although they are there to protect the consumer and not you, they are not as easily abused as they are through Google Checkout, and especially PayPal.

The big downside with having your own merchant account is cost. Rates vary and many gateways and banks have low introductory offers, which make it difficult to accurately calculate the real ongoing cost. But here is a typical example of costs after special offer periods for a typical UK business. You would need to pay the monthly charges and transaction charges of a business bank account, the monthly charges and the setup charges required by the bank for the merchant account, and the monthly and transaction charges of the gateway company. A quick calculation using a main UK bank and a well-known gateway company came to over a hundred UK pounds per month and several hundred pounds setting them up.

The other downside is that the technical requirements—how they interact with PrestaShop—of the various gateways are different and there is not always a handy module to do the job. So programming knowledge or getting your wallet out is often required.

So why would anyone use a merchant account? I already mentioned the payments are directed to your account, but the percentage charge per transaction is also usually significantly low. But, of course, you have to consider the monthly costs even before you have to take a single payment. This means merchant accounts don't usually add up for a new business.

If you are expecting a very high turnover very quickly and you want the slightly more retailer-friendly chargeback conditions, then get your wallet out and get a merchant account.

## PayPal, Google Checkout, bank wire, or cash on delivery?

PayPal and Google Checkout allow you to sign up and get trading with a few free clicks. Both companies have a PrestaShop module, which makes setting up your checkout almost as easy as adding any other module. There are some differences that will probably sway you in one direction or the other.

If you do not trust third parties then you can always use a Bank wire or Cash on delivery, but with those options the process will be slower. Anyway PrestaShop has a module if you want to offer this to your customers.

## SSL requirements

To use Google Checkout, you must use SSL. Google will not handle payments and communicate with PrestaShop without it. Shared SSL is fine, but that (as we spoke about in *Chapter 6, Security and Disaster Recovery*) does involve some technical jiggery-pokery. So a small monthly investment to buy a dedicated SSL Certificate might be necessary. PayPal, Bank wire or Cash on delivery does not require you to have an SSL Certificate.

## Cost

At the time of writing this book, Google Checkout was slightly cheaper than it is now. Both the cost per transaction and the percentage of sale value charges were slightly lower. So your handling costs with Google Checkout were lower.

## Getting your money

Google Checkout can pay you monthly or daily, as per your choice. This might sound quite good because you obviously want your money as quickly as possible. But I found out that monthly was a bit too infrequent and daily was awkward for accounting purposes. Leaving my customers' money for a whole month was awkward for maintaining cash flow and daily squirts of varying amounts of money was a major pain.

PayPal allows you to decide when to withdraw your money. So you can wait till the end of the month if you are not selling much because you are just getting started or do it weekly or more frequently, whichever is the best for you. PayPal does charge for withdrawals under £50, and, as you might expect, it takes a few days after the request to receive your funds.

## Flexibility

Google Checkout and PayPal can take payments from almost anywhere in the world. However, Google Checkout can only take the payment in your country's native currency. This means that a customer from the US could buy something from a store in France but will have to pay in Euros only.

PayPal can take payment in most major currencies, which can make your customer feel more comfortable about a purchase and will perhaps be more likely to complete it. You can specifically configure PayPal to accept other currencies or just tell PrestaShop to accept them (more on this later), and when a transaction is made with a new currency, PayPal will take the confirmation from you on whether to take it or not.

# Chargebacks

Google Checkout and PayPal offer protection to your customers. The precise terms and conditions are a bit of a minefield and I am not qualified to go into it in depth, but I can give you some feedback based on experience.

Google Checkout has a chargeback process that could be considered comparable to that of the major banks. PayPal, on the other hand, is significantly biased towards your customer. If a customer contacts PayPal and claims no delivery, PayPal will immediately freeze your funds. They will not discuss it first. If a customer complains to PayPal that goods are significantly not as described, they will do the same.

It will then be up to you to prove otherwise. You will enter into an electronic arbitration system on the PayPal website, and PayPal will decide the outcome. They will not discuss it with you. There will be no human contact and their decision is final. The frozen funds could be permanently removed from your account.

Go and have a look at www.paypalwarning.com and you'll see thousands of horror stories.

In a nutshell, you need to consider the needs of your business. If you sell the type of products that are not repeatedly purchase, are low margin, and prone to fraud, then seriously consider Google Checkout. By prone to fraud I mean the sort of goods that are easily resold for cash. Consumer electronics are a good example.

However, if you have a high-margin product where you are building a base for loyal customers who repeat their purchase, then the convenience and ease of PayPal could still be right for you. And of course, PayPal's bias towards the consumer is quite well-known. This fact could mean that the since consumers feel protected, they are more likely to shop from you and most of them, of course, are honest.

# Friendliness

If you get any technical issues with Google Checkout, you have to discuss it via e-mail. With PayPal, perhaps surprisingly, you can get technical support via telephone.

However, don't expect PayPal or Google to discuss a dispute with you. They will act in whatever way is the best for them and that will be the end of the matter.

# Conclusion

If you are wondering which one should I use, then the answer is both. So there is no best payment handler, but there will be a payment handler that suits you best.

Decide from the pros and cons and choose what is best for you. Now read on...

## Have a go hero – turning a negative into a positive

Please don't let this section put you off PayPal and Google Checkout altogether. After years of trading and having set up a dozen shops around, I still haven't moved on to a merchant account. PayPal and Google Checkout are too convenient. Just take steps to protect yourself.

Q) If you have a customer who gets a chargeback claiming non-delivery, what can you do?

A) Always get a proof of posting. If an order is not cost-effective to track, get a proof of posting. You can often claim it from the delivery service. The very fact that you have documentation of a dispute on PayPal is the evidence that a parcel has never arrived.

You can often claim up to an agreed maximum per package for the lost mail. And here is the good bit: you can often claim the retail price. So if you resupply the product to your customer and avoid a refund, you can actually make more money than if the package had got there without getting lost!

Also, by making a claim, the postal service will often investigate. If there is a person making regular fraudulent claims, you will add evidence to the case against them. I have received two feedbacks in the last few years where legal action has been taken. One action was taken against a defrauding "customer" and another was taken against an employee of the delivery service.

Check the specific details of your delivery service. If you don't like it, look for a new one. If you can't afford to lose the package, then you need to pay for tracking. If the margin is too small to pay for tracking, reconsider your prices or product range.

# Using PayPal

What follows is a really brief discussion and tutorial to get your PrestaShop connected to PayPal so that you can start taking payments. It is brief because that is all that is necessary.

## PayPal account

Visit `www.paypal.com` and you will be redirected to the PayPal site that is appropriate for your country or region. Sign up for an account if you don't already have one and make sure to choose the premier account. PayPal will want to verify your credentials with a few procedures that might take a few days. So sign up as soon as possible in order to keep off the running for passing my 7-day challenge.

## Setting up your PayPal checkout

Once you have a Premier PayPal account, you need to configure PrestaShop and your PayPal account for them to talk to each other.

# Time for action – installing the PayPal module

Here is how to do it:

1. In your PrestaShop control panel, hover on **Modules** and click on the **Payments & Gateways** option. Then install the **PayPal (Addons)** module.

2. Now click on **Configure** next to the PayPal module you just installed. Here is a screenshot of what you will see:

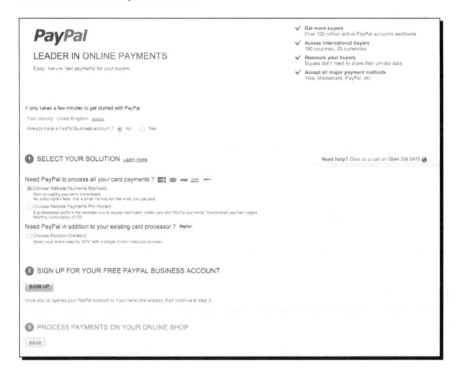

3. PayPal business e-mail simply refers to the e-mail address used on your PayPal account. So put that in there.

4. Select **No** for **Sandbox mode**. We want to do this for real.

5. Go to the main profile page by clicking on the **Profile** tab. Under the **Selling preferences** column, click on **Website Payment Preferences**. Make sure **Auto Return** and **Payment Data Transfer** are set to **Off**. These settings are turned off because PrestaShop communicates directly with PayPal to configure these options. Do not be concerned if you think these settings should be on.

## What just happened?

You told PrestaShop to use PayPal. You then gave it the payment e-mail required by PayPal. Then we clicked a few boxes on the PayPal website to make sure all is well. PrestaShop does the rest for you. How nice!

# Using Google Checkout

Here is how to do it. There is a little bit more to it than PayPal, but not much. The slightly lower fees should make the tiny bit of extra work worthwhile. Make sure you have SSL set up on your store before continuing.

Go to the Google site for your country or region. Click on **Business solutions** and then **Checkout** and sign up for a Google Checkout account if you do not already have one at `https://checkout.google.com`.

## Installing the checkout

Is your Google Checkout account open in a tab on your browser and your PrestaShop control panel in another? If it is that then we will be clicking back and forth between the two.

### Time for action – how to set up Google Checkout payments

The first thing to mention is that Google offers a "sandbox mode". This is where you can connect to Google Checkout and try everything out but in a mode where no actual financial transactions take place. This is quite handy. As our objective is to get up and running quickly, we will talk about setting up the real mode. If you want to use the sandbox mode first, the instructions are identical. You would just enter the details of your sandbox account instead of your real account. You can get a free sandbox account from `https://sandbox.google.com/checkout`.

There is nothing particularly technical here, but there are a number of steps that need to be done just right. So let's do this:

1. Hover on Modules and click on the **Payments & Gateways** on the left-hand side of the bar. Install the **gcheckout (Addons)**, and click on **Configure**.

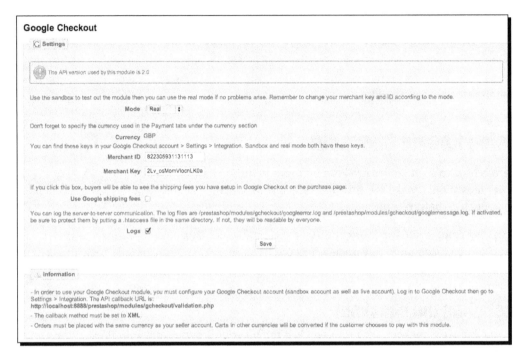

2. Set the **Mode** to **Real**.

3. On your Google Checkout account home page, in the top right corner is your **Merchant ID**. Copy and paste this into the **Merchant ID** field.

4. On your Google Checkout account, click on the **Settings** tab. Then, from the list on the left, click on **Integration**. On the right-hand side, you will see your **Merchant Key**. Copy and paste this into the **Merchant Key** field on the PrestaShop Google Checkout module configuration page.

5. Disable logging by unchecking in the **Logs** checkbox. Logging is beyond the scope of this book, and without additional action, it might present a security issue.

6. In the information box, at the bottom of the PrestaShop Google Checkout module configuration page, there is a URL in bold. This is your API callback URL. This is where Google Checkout communicates with your PrestaShop to talk about orders and payments. Copy this URL in full, including the **http** right from the end.

7. In your Google Checkout account, on the **Integration** page, paste this URL into the box labeled **API callback URL**.

8. Just below this box, check the **Notification as XML** option. This denotes the protocol that PrestaShop and Google Checkout will use to communicate.

9. Save the settings in your Google Checkout account and your PrestaShop Google Checkout module configuration page.

## What just happened?

Google Checkout and PrestaShop will now talk to each other. When a customer wants to place an order, PrestaShop will hand the last part of the process to Google Checkout who will take the money. Google Checkout will update your **Customers** and **Orders** tabs with the order details and all relevant information about the transaction.

While you are logged into Google Checkout, you might like to click on the **Financials** link on the left. Check whether your bank account details are correct and choose the frequency of payments from Google Checkout to your bank account.

## Cheque

From experience, this is probably the most common form of payment after a conventional online payment. There are a number of reasons a customer might want to pay by cheque. As an example, there are still millions of people who love the idea of the Internet to browse and research but wouldn't use their credit card online unless they could travel up the telephone wire with it to keep it safe.

Cheque is a good solution. Enable the cheque module in the usual place, click on **Configure**, and you can specify whom to make cheques payable to and where to send them. PrestaShop will communicate this information to customers wanting to use cheque as payment.

Most of my cheque orders are from customers a bit like I have described above. I have also received orders from companies where they like to be invoiced and then pay by cheque. This is a bit of a manual thing to handle but has brought the biggest, most profitable orders that any of my shops have had. It can be well worth it. You decide what is best for your business. Remember, you can change your mind with the click of a button.

## Cash on delivery

The cash on delivery module doesn't really do anything other than make the option available during checkout. You would obviously need to use a carrier that can handle cash on delivery. There are lots of potential offline security problems here but worth considering for special cases like if you are going to sell pizzas.

# Bank wire

This is where the customer makes a payment directly from their account to yours.

Click on the **Payments & Gateways** option on the left-hand side bar and then install the **Bank Wire** module. Notice that a fairly non-specific description of what is required is provided. This is because banks in different countries require different types of information to receive payments. And some banks within the same country sometimes have different requirements.

Contact your bank and find out what is required for somebody to send a payment directly to your bank account. Don't be fooled into thinking an account number and branch number (sort code) are sufficient. Very often you will need to provide BIC, SWIFT, or IBAN numbers as well.

And don't forget to check whether the payment has arrived before sending the order. So you see how this payment method could quickly become awkward or confusing to operate. I would suggest using it in special cases. Perhaps you could use this method for a really good customer who insists upon this type of payment, for a really good order, or as an occasional favor to someone who requests it.

# Sales taxes

Depending upon the country, state, or region you operate from and your type and volume of business, you will have different taxes. Also, different products have varying tax rates and exclusions as well. I hope you think it is reasonable for me to shrug responsibility for explaining what your tax rate(s) is.

PrestaShop has made it really easy to apply the appropriate tax rate regardless of the country, state, or region, if at all you have to apply tax. Find out your appropriate rate and look at this quick tutorial to set the rate in your PrestaShop.

## Time for action – setting up PrestaShop to handle sales tax

Here we go:

1. Hover on **Localization** and click on the **Taxes** subtab.
2. Click on **Add new**; enter the name and rate of tax.
3. Click on the boxes where the tax is applicable and **Save** your new tax.
4. Take a look at the screenshot below:

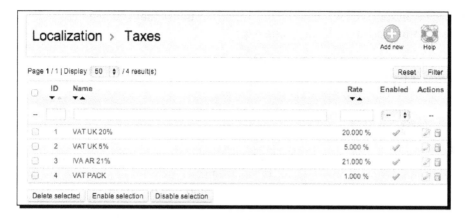

5. Click on the bin icon to delete any taxes that are not appropriate to you.

6. Finally, make sure the **Enable tax** box is ticked. Click on **Save**.

## What just happened?

It is really important to get this right. It is hard to run a business from jail. But that doesn't necessarily mean you have to get your wallet out. Most tax authorities offer free advice over the phone and face-to-face. Look for them and give them a call.

Now we can go on to explore checkout.

# One page checkout

If you want to offer to your customer a very quick payment method, then instead of having the default five steps, you should change it to one page checkout.

In one page checkout, you will have all the important things that you need to get from your customer in order to get paid only in one page.

This is a new function that is localized in the **Preferences** tab under the **General** subtab in the **Order process type** drop-down list.

# Guest checkout

It is interesting to have all your customers register on your shop but some might be a little reluctant to register on a new web. For this reason you may want to give to your customer another way to buy from your shop without any required registration.

To activate this option, you will need to hover on **Preferences** and click on **General**. Select **Yes** for the **Enable guest checkout** option and click on **Save**. Now it is not mandatory to be a registered member to buy from your store. Remember do everything keeping your customers in mind, because without them your store has no value.

# Currencies

Do you want to encourage customers from other countries to shop from your store? You could produce a foreign language version of your website to do this. This was covered in *Chapter 4, Getting More Customers*. A really quick and easy way to encourage purchases from countries other than your own is to offer products in foreign currencies.

There are three quick stages in doing this. First, we will add the currencies you want to use.

## Adding a currency

If you want to use Euros, US dollars, or GB pounds, then PrestaShop is already set up to do this. You can skip this tutorial and read about setting currency rates.

If the currency you want to use is not one of these, then read on.

## Time for action – adding a currency

Here is how to add a new currency to your PrestaShop:

1. Hover on **Localization** and click on **Currencies**.
2. Now click on the **Add new** button. The following is what you will see:

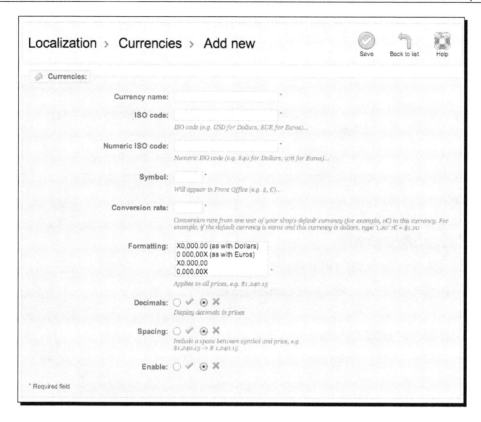

**3.** And this is how to fill out the boxes:

| Property | What to put in the box |
| --- | --- |
| **Currency name** | This is the actual name of your currency. Write the native currency as the user would expect it to find: British pounds, Euros, and so on. |
| **ISO code** | This is the internationally recognized code for currency. Dollars is USD, British pounds is GBP. To find out what is yours, visit any major news site and check out the currency rates for the day. The ISO code will be quoted there. |
| **Numeric ISO code** | This is the internationally recognized number for currency. Dollars is 840, Euros is 978. |
| **Symbol** | £, $, and so on. |
| **Conversion rate** | Leave this until the next tutorial. |
| **Formatting** | This is simple but important. When you present prices, do you want the symbol to appear before or after the price? |

| Property | What to put in the box |
|----------|------------------------|
| Decimals | For normal price formatting, click on the tick. You will have prices displayed like this $29.49. Or click on the radio button with red cross if you want to remove the decimal places and prices to be displayed like this: $49. |
| Spacing | If you want to have one space between the symbol and the price, then you have to tick this. |
| Enable | If your store is ready to sell in this currency? Yes? Then tick this option. |

Click on **Save** and read on.

## What just happened?

You now have a new currency in your store.

Read on to find out about setting the conversion rate.

## Setting currency rates

You can Google currency exchange rates or look out for them on all the major news websites. Get the exchange rates for all the currencies you wish to accept and read this quick tutorial.

## Time for action – setting a currency rate

Here we go:

1. Hover on **Localization** and then click on the **Currencies** subtab. Quickly make sure that the default currency is set correctly because all the rates we set will be used in the calculations against your default currency.

2. Click on **Update currency rates**.

3. All the conversion rates will be automatically updated by your default currency. Please use it with caution, and according the rates are provided in the market at the moment.

## What just happened?

Of course, the exchange rate is changing all the time. It is perfectly acceptable to set the rate a little higher and then just check it occasionally. We will look at auto configuring the conversion rate next. This might or might not be for you.

## Auto exchange rate updates

Go to **Localization | Currencies**. On this page there is a button to update the currencies rates. So why didn't I tell you about this 10 minutes ago, well you might ask.

Quite simply because:

♦ There is a possibility that you may want to increase the conversion rate of some or all of the currencies, in such cases, it is not self-configurable

♦ If the ISO is wrong, it won't work

♦ It can be just plain wrong

♦ Sometimes it doesn't work at all

But with these points in mind, it can be a time-saving tool. But my tip is to first check the currency rates at www.xe.com, because you can lose money if the currency rate is too low. I can auto-update occasionally with the green button **Update currency rates**, and then, if required, I can also manually raise the rate a little.

Now we can go on to explore or discuss another key aspect of the topic.

# Vouchers

Vouchers are good for a lots of things. You can sometimes give them as a refund when the customer does not qualify for a money refund. You can keep the customer's goodwill and their money. You can distribute or advertise them to encourage sales. I like to offer them as an incentive to sign up for my newsletter.

There are no ends of imaginative ways you can use gift vouchers. So let's learn how to create and distribute them now. In the next chapter, we will use gift vouchers as part of a broader campaign to launch your store and beat my 7-day challenge of opening your store and getting your first sale within seven days.

## Creating a voucher

First of all, we need to define the parameters of our voucher—when it can be used, who can use it, how much, and a bit more as well.

# Time for action – creating a voucher

Follow this quick tutorial to create a voucher:

1.  Hover on **Price Rules** and click on **Cart Rules**.

2.  Now click on **Add new** and you will see the voucher creation screen. A screenshot followed by a table of what to put where follows:

3.  And this is how to fill out the boxes:

| Voucher option | Explanation |
| --- | --- |
| **Name** | The name that you want to give to your Voucher, it will be like an identification. |
| **Description** | This field is just for you. But it is a good practice to add some information for the future reference to know what you did. |
| **Code** | This is the code that must be entered at the checkout by the customer in order to get the discount. |
| | It is worth giving meaningful names to your vouchers so that you can track their usage and success using PrestaShop statistics features. |
| | But not too long because that makes it awkward for your customers to use. |
| | Perhaps JAN20% or AMMO5%. You get the idea. |
| | PrestaShop can also auto generate a random code if you like. |

| Voucher option | Explanation |
| --- | --- |
| Partial use | If you want to facilitate your customer by allowing him to use a part of the voucher because the checkout is lower than the value of the voucher, then you need to tick this. |
| Priority | If a customer has a different voucher, then the voucher with a lower number will be the valid one. |
| Status | Tick if it is active. |
| Limit to a single customer | If you leave this field blank, then the voucher will be available for every customer but if you want to restrict the voucher to several customers, you will need to add their e-mail here. |
| Valid | Voucher period. |
| Minimum amount | Define the minimum order value this voucher can be used for or leave blank for no restriction. This might be particularly relevant for vouchers with a cash discount. |
| Total available | If you want to offer this voucher just for the specific amount of first person users who can use this voucher. |
| Total available for each user | The number of times that a customer can use this voucher. |
| Free shipping | If you want to add free shipping to the voucher, you have to tick this option. |
| Apply a discount | In this field you can add a discount in percent or in amount. Select your needs. |
| Apply discount to | The voucher can be applicable only to a specific product, cheapest product or selected products. |
| Send a free gift | Tick this if you want to add free gift in this voucher. |

Click on the **Save** button and move on.

## What just happened?

Now that you have a voucher, people can enter the voucher code during the checkout process and get the discount you specified. PrestaShop makes sure all your specifications, such as valid dates and quantity per user, are adhered to. If you suddenly realize that a mistake has been made, you can quickly disable the voucher.

But how does your customer know about the voucher?

# Giving the vouchers to your customer

To give a voucher to a customer, all you have to do is give them the code. PrestaShop can then take care of the details based on the parameters you defined when creating the voucher. But distribution of vouchers goes a little bit deeper.

I like to create a structure of vouchers for different customers to make as many purchases as possible. Consider running a number of voucher promotions simultaneously. I will give you an example of a voucher structure in a moment, but obviously you must consider what would work and be profitable to your business. Hopefully, my example will give you some ideas if not the precise format for a multi-voucher promotion.

◆ **5 percent off on everything**: A small percentage of amount available to absolutely everyone on a one-off basis. Distribute this on relevant forums, social media, your home page, and on Google AdWords. There's more in the next chapter about these and other promotional ideas.

◆ **10 percent off on everything**: Consider a bigger, more significant, one-off discount for signing up to your newsletter. It is often okay to give away a bit more of your profit in return for constant contact with your customer. Remember the value of e-mail marketing when you do it right. You could get multiple sales without any discount if your customer signs up for and enjoys your newsletters.

◆ **Free shipping when you spend**: Consider offering free shipping, perhaps permanently, in return for larger-than-average orders. Look at or estimate your customers' average spend per order. Then consider a value at which to offer free shipping that encourages customers to put an extra item or three in their basket. Remember to have lots of great add-on and accessory options. You can advertise this anywhere and everywhere.

◆ **10 percent off category X**: Always keep promoting something for customers who don't qualify or have already used other vouchers. A discount on a specific category will encourage customers to make additional purchases at the same time as non-discounted ones.

Whatever you decide is best for your shop—take your time to do the math. There is no point selling anything if you don't make what you need.

# Shipping options

Shipping is a surprisingly wide and deep topic. When I opened my first e-commerce store, I was very surprised at the complexity involved in adding a shipping charge to an order. So here are a couple of ways you might be able to avoid any complexity-not to save us a few minutes or hours configuring your shipping options because if your specific business situation demands it, then that is what you obviously have to do. But if even we are baffled by the vast array of shipping configurations, then what will our customers think? Will it lose us some customers?

In the vast majority (but not all of my stores), I use one of the two following super-simple shipping configurations. If one of these work for you, then I recommend using it. If not, what follows from my super-simple shipping configurations are a summary of the PrestaShop shipping configuration options.

# Super-simple shipping configuration options

Is it possible to build the cost of shipping within your product range specifically? I have heard arguments against this because it can make the product look more expensive without close examination. My view is that customers are not stupid. As long as you make it plain and shout about the fact that shipping is included in all your prices, then customers will actually appreciate the upfront cost. It can even be a really great feature of your store. 90 percent of my stores are all products and free delivery on all products.

♦ To configure free shipping in PrestaShop, click on the **Shipping** tab and change all the figures you see in the following screenshot to zero and save it:

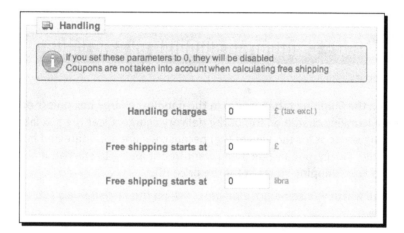

♦ Another option is to configure PrestaShop for free shipping as earlier, and then consider adding a flat postage rate for any product. This can be done through the same mechanism shown previously by changing the handling charges to whatever you want your flat fee to be and then changing **Free shipping starts at** to 0. So if you don't want to load the shipping cost onto the product but want to keep things super simple, you can add a flat fee onto every purchase.

# Common shipping scenarios

The PrestaShop shipping configuration options does a good job of removing some of the complexity of shipping configuration. However, necessarily it is still very in-depth and it could easily take up a couple of chapters on its own.

My objective here is to show you exactly how to configure a couple of common scenarios. So if you like, skip ahead and follow the tutorial that is most appropriate for you. If, on the other hand, you want a deep and full explanation before you decide, then read all the different options because, in the last section on configuring shipping, *Shipping configuration in depth*, I will give you some good ideas on how to do almost anything you like.

If you are looking to set up a shop that sells products of varied values and weights to different geographic locations and want to vary the shipping cost according to all of these factors, then read the three specific scenarios as an introduction and then study the *Shipping configuration in depth* section, including the Bikes4u case study.

As promised, let's start with some relatively simple and common scenarios.

## Shipping calculated by sale value

This method gives you the flexibility to define the price range. The ranges can be as narrow or as wide as you like. You can then, with a few clicks, assign a shipping price to each range. PrestaShop will then charge customers for shipping according to the total value of their order.

## Time for action – configuring shipping by sale value

This is how to do it:

1. Click on the **Shipping** tab. Put zero in the handling charge box unless of course you want a handling charge on top of the delivery charge. Clear the box labeled **Free shipping starts at** for the weight (**kg**) because we are not interested in weight at this stage. Finally, put a value if you want free shipping to start at, if any, in the box labeled **Free shipping starts at** for the price (**€**).

2. Now we will define some price ranges. Click on the **Price Ranges** subtab and then on **Add new**.

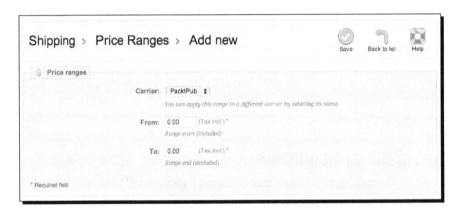

3. Type in the starting value of your first order value price range. Almost certainly the **From** price will be **0**. Enter the upper limit of the first range. So if you wanted to charge a specific amount of shipping for orders from 0.01 to 49.99, enter the value 50.00. Click on **Save**.

4. Now click on **Add new** again. Enter the starting value of your range in the **From** box. This should be the same as the **To** value from the previous range. This is because the actual value you enter in the **From** field is inclusive, but the value you enter in the **To** field is not inclusive. So if you define the second range as **From: 50** and **To: 100** then the following will apply. All orders up to 49.99 will be in price range one and all orders from 50.00 to 99.99 will be in price range two. Click on **Save** when you're done.

5. Define as many ranges as you need. On the last range make the **To** figure higher than you expect an order to ever be. This is the way you will have to define a range for any potential order. If, in the Step 1, you added a value, where you offer a free shipping, then your highest orders should have that free shipping range.

6. Now that we have created some ranges, we will now assign a shipping cost to each range.

7. Click on the **Shipping** tab and scroll to the bottom of the page. You can view a summary of the ranges you just made. In my following example, I used three ranges: **$0 to $50, $50 to $100**, and **$100 to 250$**.

8. Simply enter the delivery price of each order value range and click on **Save**.

9. Go and put a few things in your basket and see how it works.

## What just happened?

You have now defined your shipping costs based on the value of the customer's order. You can define the ranges as widely or as narrowly as you like.

## Configuring shipping by weight

This method gives you the flexibility to define ranges of weight. The ranges can be as narrow or as wide as you like. You can then, with a few clicks, assign a shipping price to each range of order weight. PrestaShop will then charge customers for shipping according to the total weight of their order.

## Time for action – how to configure shipping by weight

The first thing to do is to tell PrestaShop the weight of each of your products so that it can sum it up together. So let's get on with it:

1. During the setup of your products, we discussed the weight property in the product configuration page. If you didn't define the weight then but now if you have decided to calculate shipping by weight, then click back into your products and configure the weight before continuing.

2. Click on the **Shipping** tab. Put zero in the handling charge box unless of course you want a handling charge on top of the delivery charge. Clear the box labeled **Free shipping starts at** for the price because we are not interested in order price in this tutorial. Finally, put a weight you want free shipping to start at, if any, in the box labeled **Free shipping starts at** for the weight.

3. Now we will define some weight ranges. Click on the **Weight ranges** subtab and then on **Add new**.

4. Type in the starting value of your first order weight range. Almost certainly the value of **From** weight will be **0**. Enter the upper limit of the first range. So if you wanted to charge a specific amount of shipping for orders from 0.01 kg to 4.99 kg, enter the value **5.00**. Click on **Save**.

5. Now click on **Add new** again. Enter the starting value of your range in the **From** box. This should be the same as the **To** value from the previous range. This is because the actual value you enter in the **From** field is inclusive but the value you enter in the **To** field is not inclusive. So if you define the second range as **From: 5** and **To: 10**, then the following will apply. All orders weighing up to 4.99 kg will be in price range one and all orders from 5.00 up to 9.99 will be in price range two. Click on **Save** when you're done.

6. Define as many ranges as you need to. On the last range, make the **To** figure higher than you expect an order to ever be. This way you will have defined a range for any potential order. However, if, in Step 1, you entered a value where free shipping starts, then your highest ranges **To** value should equal the value at which free shipping starts.

7. Now that we have created some ranges, we will assign a shipping cost to each range.

8. Click on the **Shipping** tab and scroll to the bottom of the page. Make sure that **According to total weight** is selected. You can then view a summary of the ranges you just made.

9. Simply enter the delivery price of each weight range and click on **Save**.

10. Go and put a few things in your basket and see how it works.

## What just happened?

You have defined your shipping costs based on the weight of your customer's order.

Now we can go on to explore the PrestaShop shipping configuration options in more depth.

## Shipping configuration in depth

Think about this scenario.

Bikes4u is the web outlet for a major bikes reseller. Bikes4u has a very wide range of bikes, from children to professional bikers.

So the need for a more flexible shipping solution is apparent. For example, a private customer ordering a mountain bike to be delivered will raise varied different costs depending upon the place of delivery.

If you also consider that the products of similar weights could actually cost varied different amounts. This is because we need to consider the type and also the manner of their delivery needs to be catered. Perhaps a wheel compared to a pedal. Clearly, the latter needs much more sophisticated and costly transport.

Can PrestaShop be configured to offer a solution?

Part of the solution lies in offering multiple shipping options. It is possible to have multiple carriers and then define each carrier to use a different shipping method.

You can create an extra carrier. Hover on **Shipping**, then click on **Carriers**, and then on **Add new**.

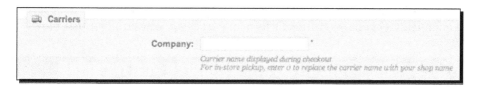

Notice the top field in the previous form—**Company**. This is not necessarily for the actual company, it can also be for a description of the service. For example, in the Bikes4u, we could create a carrier called "Large parcels". This enables us to make it clear to our customers what the carrier is for. We can then define order value or weight ranges specific to this carrier. This is achieved after creating our new carrier by defining a weight or order value range in the normal way but selecting our new carrier in the drop-down box as we do so.

Notice also in the **Add new carrier** form that the option to define availability by continent. So you could create multiple carriers with different price or weight ranges, perhaps called "Small pieces Europe", "Small pieces Africa", and so on.

As you can see things can get complicated. Forget Bikes4u for a moment and consider a large online retailer like Amazon. Think about the vast range of weights, order values, product types, and destinations, not to mention the choice of different speeds within all these other possibilities.

The key to a successful shipping configuration, like that on Amazon, when a very simple price, weight, flat fee, or free model will not do, is planning. If you must introduce multiple carriers, think carefully about what to call them and how to configure them, because your customers, not us, need to understand them in order to spend money.

If it is not necessary to create new carriers in PrestaShop, then don't. Let's suppose we use regular mail for order weights up to x and a courier for x and over. Do we need to create two carriers in PrestaShop? The answer is that if a single carrier, perhaps "Our carrier", can have weight ranges defined that charge what we need to, then don't create a new carrier in PrestaShop. A simple explanation of when you use regular mail and when you use a courier on your **Delivery and Returns** page would probably be much better.

The new and important functionality in PrestaShop 1.5 is the fact that you can assign different carriers to every single product. This is really a handy feature when dealing with different kinds of products.

# Gift wrapping and recycled packaging

On top of all these shipping options, there are two more. They can be both money makers and credibility builders. If you offer a product suitable to be a gift, why not offer a gift wrapping service and charge for it? If you have a product that is available in full packaging or a more minimalist, environment-friendly form of packaging, why not offer that too?

## Time for action – setting up gift wrapping and recycled packaging options

Here is how to do it.

1. Hover on the **Preferences** tab and click on **Orders**.

2. Scroll down to what you can see in the following screenshot.

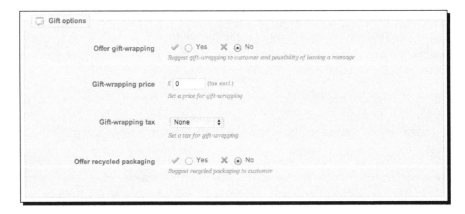

3.  Click on **Yes** or **No** for gift wrapping.

4.  Enter a price for the service.

5.  Enter a tax rate, if any.

6.  Click on **Yes** or **No** to **Offer recycled packaging**.

## What just happened?

By offering gift wrapping and recycled packaging, you can increase your turnover, and please your customers. This can all be done at the same time with just a couple of clicks.

## Pop quiz – a refresher

Q1. How does SSL make your password safer?

1.  Because all the banks use this way

2.  It is the Super Secure Login mode

3.  Because it is a protocol for encrypting information over the Internet

Q2. How are your customers' credit card details protected when using PayPal, even if you don't use SSL?

1.  PayPal is like a bank, for that the use the Super Secure Login mode

2.  Because, when the customers use the PayPal payment gateway, they automatically jump to the PayPal servers

3.  That only happens if it is selected in the PayPal properties

# Your PrestaShop so far

Phew, this chapter was a big one! But it is worth knowing how advanced and in-depth your options are.

Are you starting to get a little bit excited? Your shop is ready. It is connected and configured for real customers. Goodbye 9-5, hello e-commerce business.

# Summary

We learned a lot in this chapter about checkouts, currencies, taxes, and shipping.

Specifically, we covered:

◆ How to choose and connect the best payment provider for your business

◆ Some alternate payment methods

◆ How to take multiple currencies and configure sales taxes

◆ How to set up simple and efficient shipping options

Now that we've reached this stage, we will do a few quick checks on your checkout, get some family/friends' sales to make your shop look used, and then give the final push to your first small wave of real customers. All this and more will be covered in *Chapter 8, Ready to Sell*.

# 8
# Ready to Sell

*This chapter is all about final preparations. It's a quick dry run through the process of making a purchase, followed by the first steps in a diverse marketing campaign that we will cover more in detail in the next chapter.*

In this chapter, we shall:

- Create a customer account and place an order
- Look at the PrestaShop customer loyalty scheme
- Look at how to get some feedback on your products using the PrestaShop Product Comments module
- Tell the search engines about your cool new shop
- Look at a multi-pronged marketing campaign, which includes vouchers and social media
- Cover some functionality of the Customers and Orders tabs that we haven't already covered

So let's get on with it.

Before we look at the first element of the campaign, let's make sure that everything is working properly, such as checkouts and shipping, because we will look unprofessional in front of our customers if these are not working properly.

First of all, let's get ourselves a customer. Here you will need the goodwill of a friend or relative. We are going to ask them to make a purchase. You can obviously refund the purchase once the transaction is complete. I am also going to suggest that you lend or give away some of your products for them to use. The reasons for this will become clear as we proceed through the chapter.

# Creating an account and placing an order

You can create an account on behalf of your willing volunteer or you can ask them to create it for themselves. The important thing for us here is to pay close attention to the details of the sign up process. We are looking to see whether we have missed something. Does it look easy and intuitive? If your willing volunteer is doing the form filling, did he or she find it straightforward?

## Time for action – creating an account and placing an order

Here's how to do it. I will go through this tutorial as if you are doing the clicking.

1. Browse through your store and add a couple of products to your cart. Click on the cart link and see what it looks like. Does it all look straightforward and intuitive to you?

2. Click on the **Check out** button and create an account when you are prompted to do so.

3. Click on the **Next** button and review the shipping summary page. Does it appear as expected, with the right shipping options? If it does, click on **Next**.

4. Select one of the payment options: PayPal, Google Checkout, or any other option that you have set up. If you have chosen to offer the cheque, bank wire, or cash on delivery payment methods, then I suggest that you do not choose them here. It will be useful (as we will see later in the chapter) to see how PrestaShop integrates with your chosen payment provider; we will discuss how to handle orders as well.

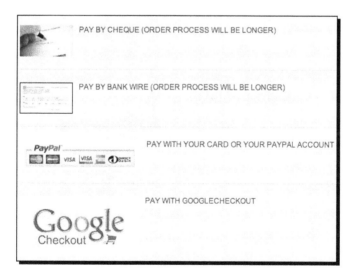

5. Complete the transaction through your preferred payment provider.

## *What just happened?*

Now we know that the whole process is up and working. We understand first hand what our customers need to do in order to spend money in our store. We are now much better placed to serve them and turn them into long-term, big spenders. We will use this account to do a few things in this chapter.

Let's look at a PrestaShop feature to encourage repeat business.

If you need to change/add fields for the customer registration form, we can always edit it in our back office.

# Repeat business with a customer loyalty scheme

The customer loyalty scheme is great. If you have enough profit margins in your products, consider giving a little bit back to your customers in return for some repeat purchases. This works especially well if your customers have lots of stores to choose from and you sell repeatedly purchased items.

The best way to learn about how the loyalty scheme works is by setting it up.

## Time for action – setting up your loyalty scheme

Here's what to do:

1. Click on the **Modules** tab and scroll down to the **Customer loyalty and rewards** scheme. Install this module.

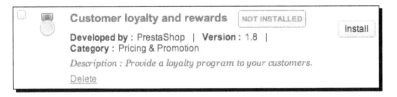

2. Click on **Configure**. You will see something similar to the following screenshot:

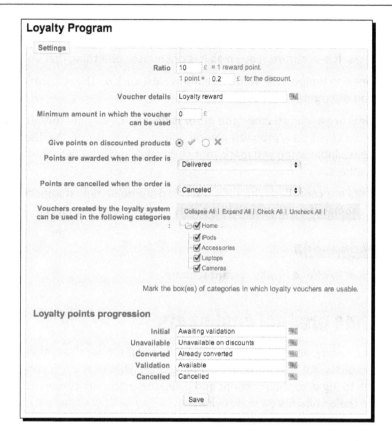

**3.** Most of the fields can be left as they are, with their default values. Here is an explanation of the interesting or important ones. First, in the **Ratio** field, enter the number of US dollars ($), British pounds sterling (£), or Euros that a customer must spend to earn a point.

**4.** Underneath this field, you will have to enter the value of a single point as the decimal fraction of your chosen unit of currency. Do the math carefully for this value. For example, if you leave in the default values of $10 per point and the value at 0.2 per point, then for every $10 your customer spends, they will get 20 cents. If this is not generous enough, you can reduce the required spending per point, say, to 5. Then they would get 20 cents for every $5 spent. Or you can make it your strategy to encourage a high average spend and then reward it by being a bit more generous. You can make the customer spend $50 per point but then give them a $5 value. Think carefully about what will work for you.

5. Enter what you want the voucher to be called in the **Voucher details** field. Leave it at `Loyalty reward`, or call it something else such as `Fluff points` or `Thanks vouchers`. It is arbitrary, leave it as it is or choose something that you like.

6. If you need to temporarily stop discounting, just click on the red cross next to **Give points on discounted products**.

7. The **Points are awarded when the order is** field is self-explanatory. The default value of `Delivered` is probably a good option. It means that the discount will become available when you mark your customer's order as delivered. But you can choose others.

8. The **Points are cancelled when the order is** drop-down field is important because it stops customers from accumulating points when they get refunds or cancel an order.

## What just happened?

You now know how to offer a loyalty reward scheme.

# Getting some product comments

You now have somebody who is using your products, and it is time to ask them what they think of these products. You can also ask for feedback on what they think about your store. You can ask them to log in to their account and leave some product comments. Alternatively, you could create the comments on their behalf.

## All about comments

I strongly recommend that you do not invent comments. Such comments are really easy to spot and obviously show the lack of integrity. This is not the path we want to start on, right at the beginning of our new business. However, filling out some comments on behalf of a genuine user of our products is probably fine.

The benefit of this is, you will again get to see how the process works, and just as importantly, your future customers will have comments to view. This makes your site look more established as well as being useful and reassuring to a customer for the purpose of making decisions.

## How to get some product comments

Get the feedback of your willing volunteer. Then follow this quick guide.

# Time for action – getting some feedback for your products

This is really easy.

1. First of all, we need to enable product comments. Of course, if you think product comments are not suitable for your store, then you don't have to do this. However, the benefits are great so think carefully before skipping this guide. Log in to your admin control panel.

2. Click on the **Modules** tab, and install the **Product Comments** tab. Now click on **Configure**, next to the module you have just installed.

You will see the following screenshot when you click on **Configure**:

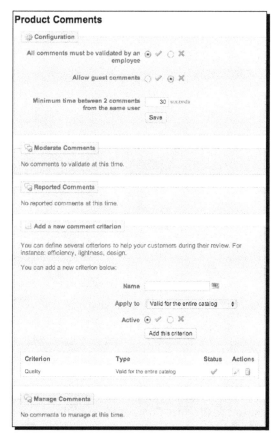

**3.** Select whether you want to validate comments before publishing them. This option is useful if you are nervous about what people might say.

**4.** The next two options for **Criterion** are optional. For each product, you can create a grading criterion. Let me explain. Your customer will be able to choose upto five stars. You can suggest and specify a criterion for these stars (for example, **Please choose 1 star for poor or 5 stars for great**). You can then assign specific criteria to specific products in the next box. As I said, this step is not necessary; however, if you have a product range that would benefit from a specific criterion, then specify it here (for example, a site such as `Bikes4U.com` would use **Weight** or **Quality**).

**5.** Click on **Save** and visit your shop front. Browse to the first product you want to leave a comment for. Notice the new tab at the bottom of the screen. Click on it.

**6.** Leave a rating in stars (be honest) and a product comment. Click on **Send**.

**7.** Now go back to your admin control panel, click on the **Modules** tab, and then click on **Configure** next to the **Product Comments** module.

**8.** Notice that you can approve or delete any of the comments. Obviously, it is not a good practice to delete a comment just because it is imperfect. However, if the comments are unfair, untrue, or abusive, then I would say that you have complete liberty to delete them. Approve your comment, and then go back to the products page to see the effect on the **Comments** tab.

**9.** Create and approve as many comments as you can.

## What just happened?

You now know the experience your customers will have when writing comments, and you also have a good, ethical way to get some comments on your store before real customers start shopping.

Now we will look at adding a juicy incentive for all your visitors.

# Putting up a discount voucher on the front page

We already know how to make a voucher. Here we will create a voucher for a very specific purpose: getting some sales as soon as possible and winning my 7-day challenge.

## Creating the voucher (reminder)

Vouchers appear on the **Price Rules** tab. The things to consider here are the precise values for which you will create your vouchers.

I would suggest a percentage rather than a cash value, because we don't know what sort of order values we might get. I would suggest a modest percentage, but one big enough to be enticing—maybe 10 percent, if your profit margin can take it.

Set the total quantity quite high. Then the vouchers will continue to be available until you disable them. Define a start and an end date for the vouchers—I would suggest maybe a month.

I would enter something like `Store opening offer` for the voucher description and a simple, memorable code for the customer to enter during checkout.

## Showcasing the voucher

Here I am assuming you have already created your voucher using the guidance provided in the previous section or (if necessary) by referring to the content in the previous chapter.

## Time for action – putting your voucher on the home page

Do you remember the **Home text editor** module? We will use it here to showcase your opening offer voucher.

*1.* Click on the **Modules** tab, scroll down to **Home text editor**, and click on **Configure**.

*2.* Make sure to put your voucher, as described next, before the fold. That is, when a visitor arrives at your home page, they should be able to see it without having to scroll through the page.

*3.* I suggest entering a very short introduction to the voucher (probably one sentence only, such as **Have a look at this great opening offer**). Then, below that, I recommend using a graphic of a gift voucher. If you're feeling arty, you could create one in GIMP. If not, visit `www.dreamstime.com` and pick up a high quality, enticing voucher graphic for around US $1. Below this graphic, in big bold letters, enter the voucher code.

*4.* Click on the **Update the editor** button and visit your home page to check and approve of the layout.

## What just happened?

Everyone who visits your home page now has a reason to explore further—a discount.

We now have a great shop. We know it works, we have entered comments to make it look used, and we have an enticing, special opening offer. It is time to tell the world that we are here.

# Registering with the search engines

Some of the search engines might have found you already. Certainly, once other sites start to link to you, they would find you anyway. However, just to be absolutely sure, we need to ensure that we are considered for inclusion with all of the major search engines. We will spend a few minutes registering with them.

## Registering

Registering with these major search engines will mean you have covered over 95 percent of all searches. Spend time registering with the smaller ones later if you like, but at this stage, this is more than sufficient.

## Time for action – registering with the search engines

We will look at Google first, then Bing and Yahoo!.

1.  Go to `http://www.google.com/addurl/` and fill out the simple form. Also consider signing up for **Google Webmaster Tools**, and explore the options and statistics that it provides.

2.  For Bing, you need to visit `http://www.bing.com/toolbox/webmaster`; you will need a Windows Live ID. If you don't already have one, you can create one for free.

3.  Yahoo! has merged with Bing, so if you did the previous step, this one has been done too.

### What just happened?

You might get your site indexed immediately, or it might take months. Don't worry too much about it because there is no way to influence the search giants other than by creating great, unique content. And, of course, we have already done that.

Now let's look at getting your first sale.

# Marketing your site

The information in this part of the chapter is designed to be digested in full and used fairly simultaneously. If you want to act on each section individually, to dip your toe in, that's fine, but my intention is to help you start a campaign that brings you your first wave of paying customers.

It is also important to realize that the brief burst of activity described here is not the end of the matter. We will look at some ways in which you can get visitors and links to your site. However, be sure to read *Chapter 9, Go... to the Future* to turn what you do here into an ongoing, effective campaign.

Let's get on with it then.

# How to write good posts

You do not necessarily have to be an expert in your field, as most forums cater to users of many skill levels. However, it is very important to try to pretend that you are an expert even if you are not; if you do consider yourself an expert, do not overstate your level of knowledge.

## Write at your skill level

You will certainly damage your reputation if you attempt to come across as more of an expert than you really are. So if you don't fully understand a topic of conversation, but want to join in any way, come clean about your level of knowledge. For example, you could start a reply to a post with "I'm no expert but if...". You can give an opinion, even one that disagrees with the post but in which you are hinting that you could be wrong. If you're right, you will come across as polite, and if you're wrong, you will not be the target of potentially embarrassing replies.

## Social share buttons

Using social networks is the easiest way in which you can approach your future customers because then everyone can share your shop or certain items from your shop on Twitter or Facebook.

I recommend **Beetailer Widget**. You can download it at `http://addons.prestashop.com/en/social-commerce-facebook-prestashop-modules/2928-beetailer-widget-facebook-plugins-and-twitter-integration.html`.

## Criticism

People don't like being criticized. If you absolutely must point out that somebody is wrong, do so in a very delicate manner.

## Don't shamelessly promote yourself

If you sign up for a forum and then post "Hi, come and check out my new bike shop", you will be doomed to fail. At the very least, other members will make a mental note of the fact that you are a self-promoter and will take what you say with caution. What's even more likely is that your post will be removed and you might have your account deleted.

The best way to promote your business is to get involved in conversations about your industry, which you should be genuinely interested in. You will gain respect, and you never know when the conversation might naturally take a course towards an opportunity to mention your shop. Take the opportunity if it arises, but don't keep mentioning it unless the conversation makes it completely natural to do so.

If the forum allows it and it is natural to do so (as discussed earlier), include a link to your site (if not, your web address would suffice).

The one exception to all of these rules is when the forum has a category specifically intended for promoting your business.

So what is the point of all these conversations if you never, or rarely, get the opportunity to shout out about your PrestaShop site?

# Promoting your store using social media

Social media, at the moment at least, seems to be the big thing on the Web. There are many social media sites that allow anybody to join and communicate with millions of members. This is obviously an opportunity that is not to be missed. However, it is very easy to end up on the wrong path. It is very easy to waste time, and it is also possible to do your business more harm than good.

To address these potential pitfalls and to make sure you get the most benefit possible with the smallest investment of time, I have created a whirlwind guide to two of the biggest social media sites. I aim going to point out the biggest benefits of each and the most likely stumbling blocks, as well as some specific methods and actions that work on each platform.

If you want results in as short a time as possible, then read on.

## Twitter

Twitter is my favorite because it is so quick and easy. The very nature of Twitter makes it really easy for you to build your network. On Twitter, you build a team of "followers". You can also be a follower of other Twitter users. If you want significant, fast results, Twitter could be for you. However, as with all social media relationships, quality informational content (called tweets in this case) is still vital to lasting success. Here are some quick dos and don'ts.

### Branding your profile

Make sure that your Twitter page represents your brand and products well, and has your domain name boldly shown. Also, in the settings, be sure to link to your home page.

## Following others

It is a good idea to follow some other Twitter profiles. This is the essence of a network on Twitter. If you want people to read your information and follow your links in your tweets, then you need people to follow you. However, there are many advantages to following others.

For example, you can get really fantastic, really topical information by following people interested in and knowledgeable about your industry. In the unlikely event that there is nobody on Twitter who fits the bill, you have a massive opportunity to become that person. Another advantage of following a respected and popular user is that you can comment on their tweets. This, along with the fact that you appear in their list of followers, means that more people have a chance of finding you. The holy grail of this type of relationship is when the respected user decides to follow you! And when they start replying to your tweets, it will bring even more viewers and potential new followers to your Twitter home page.

## A lightning guide to tweeting

Every tweet should be meaningful on its own or add something to the conversation. Just remember that everything you say is public. If you send a direct message, then even that could be repeated publicly. Don't reveal anything private about yourself, and if you want to be popular on Twitter, don't spoil anybody else's day by revealing private information about them.

### Regular tweets

Just answer the question, "What are you doing now?" Make sure you are tweeting relevant industry information: "I am considering a new range of teddy bears for my shop. Do I want the giant golden teddy? Or is small best?".

A quick glance at almost any twitterer, and you will see that they tweet a lot more than just answering the question, "What are you doing now?". Make up your own questions and answer them, for example, "What is the very latest innovation in your industry?" Answer the question and, most importantly, give your opinion about it in a single tweet.

It takes some refining of your text, but it can almost always be done. What is the biggest upcoming event in your industry and what do you think about it? For example: "Looking forward to the teddy bears annual convention this fall—no way am I going to miss it— anyone else coming?" Asking a question begs for a reply. And as we know, replies are good for business. There is no end of topics that can be thought up for even the smallest niche. Sometimes the topic could be an ongoing one that could justify many tweets over time. For example: "Just looking into how these wonderful Russian teddy bears are manufactured. Did you know they start with stuffing made from Siberian wool? "The lining is hand stitched blah blah...", and so on. You get the idea. Never lose focus on how to make it relevant for your audience. Be consistent, not too frequent, and keep it uncommercial (see the *Sales tweets* section a bit further on).

## What's your frequency Kenneth?

What tweeting frequency is right for you will depend upon how frequently things change and how dynamic your industry is. Test out different frequencies and look at what popular people in your industry are doing. What you can do, quite legitimately, is link to a very closely related article on your website. This is perfectly acceptable and would not put off followers. Just make sure that the article you link to is entirely relevant and not a product page.

## Broadcasting

All your regular tweets should be relevant and personal. So even when talking about an event, for example, the focus is on you and how the event relates to you. The exception to this rule is when you just want to broadcast something really significant. For example, "Fire at Siberian stuffing plant kills three and puts teddy production back by six months".

This is a tweet that people might be interested in, but something that is not personal. And, if the timing is right, broadcast tweets will get you lots of attention. But they should not be the standard format for your tweets. Being impersonal all the time is uninteresting. Pick your broadcast tweets carefully and make sure they are relevant and topical, even more so than your regular tweets.

## Humor

If you've got it, flaunt it. Jokes are great, and there are plenty of jokes on Twitter. A good joke can keep your followers keen. But if you haven't got it, it's probably best to leave the jokes to someone else.

## Questions

Questions are great. Asking for peoples' opinions often provokes a reply and an appearance on someone else's timeline. By all means ask for help, but keep it occasional. The best type of question is one that asks for opinions. If you ask for an opinion, you can get responses without being socially indebted. Also, if you are lucky (or smart), you might provoke a discussion, lots of replies, and the publicity that goes with it. The sorts of questions that you can ask are almost limitless. Ask about industry, business, products events, personalities, organizations, or anything else relevant. Ask for feedback on a new article, product, or site layout. Almost anything is valid.

## Achievements and events

Done something great, new, or interesting? Think your followers will care? Then tweet it. Attended an industry event, visited a competitor's store/site, had a nice lunch, tweet it all. Anything is valid. Just remember that it must be worth reading. So if you regularly tweet valid information about your field of expertise, then the occasional, informal nicety is cool and a nice contrast. But don't overdo the trivial.

## Replying and retweeting

Can't think of anything to say? No problem. Find somebody who can. Search for the phrases you are interested in and find something relevant to post a reply to. This will tell all your followers what you are looking at. And who knows, the other person's tweet might inspire something original from you. And if you're really stuck, just retweet (copy) someone's message. Be sure to give credit to the other person. You can do this by adding `RT @otherpersonstwitterusername` to the beginning of the message.

## Sales tweets

The simplest and most subtle way of promoting your site is by adding a link to your home page with your occasional tweets. The tweet does not have to suggest a purchase or promote a product; it should simply say what you want to say and link to your home page so that people can click on it and see what you are all about.

A more direct method, but still fairly subtle, is to ask people for an opinion on a very specific aspect of a product or service. Ask for feedback on the product itself, or the way in which you have described or photographed it. You could ask people for their suggestions on a selling price, or just ask "How much would you pay for this teddy?".

You can do this with an existing range or use the same process to get feedback on potential, new ranges before you purchase stock. This could generate some useful feedback and even some pre-orders.

If you're really stuck, promote your business by offering discount vouchers. Consider this very carefully before doing it, because it needs to be financially viable.

Tell your followers about special offers, but be careful. If you're sending out a tweet to a group of trusting followers, be absolutely sure that it is genuinely and undeniably special! If it isn't, you will lose credibility and probably followers as well. There are loads of people on Twitter sending out "special offer" tweets that have links to rubbish, spam, or pornography. Don't get tarred with the same brush.

## Twitter summary

Build a following by following other quality users, interacting with them, and by sending your own quality tweets. You can probably see a trend developing here; it's the same with all web content—quality and useful content—don't ram your products (too hard) down people's throats.

Also, you can explore your Twitter community at `www.socialbro.com`.

# Facebook

Facebook is more technically endowed than Twitter. The features and fancy gadgets on Facebook are far too numerous to go into any greater depth. However, there are a few really key places you can market yourself and one really important thing you must never do on Facebook.

## Avoid spamming

Whenever you post something to your wall or send any other type of message, all of the recipients have the option to report it as spam. If too many people do this, your Facebook account is likely to get deleted.

So although I do recommend building your network as wide as possible, I don't recommend sending commercial messages to your entire group. However, there are a number of communication channels where you can get a bit commercial and where you shouldn't get reported for spam. In addition, anyone in your social group will be able to see these channels when they look at your Facebook profile.

Therefore, by building the biggest network possible but only marketing through very specific, targeted channels, you can avoid the spam problem and reach a wider, targeted audience. A brief discussion of my top three Facebook features for targeted communication now follows.

## Start a group

There is a group for just about everything on Facebook. Have a look at www.facebook.com/groups. You can use the search by typing in a keyword and looking for a very specific group or click on **Browse Groups** to see the huge range, volume, and diversity of groups. Click on **Browse Groups** and we will explore a little.

Anybody can create a group, and the group could be targeted at anything. When a group is created, its creator defines certain criteria. This includes whether the group is open, closed, or secret. If a group is open, (you guessed it) you can join it. If it is closed, you will have to put in a request to join it; if it is a secret group, you will know nothing about it unless you are a member.

Secret groups are all cool and funky for conversing with college buddies but have limited use in the world of marketing, so we will say no more about them. When you visit a group page, you will be able to see what they are all about and then decide whether you want to join one.

Join groups relevant to your industry, and make new friends once you join in. Start your own group as a really powerful, targeted marketing channel.

## Start an event

Events are exactly what they say. Anybody can create an event page. The event page can then be visited by Facebook members, and they can interact with it. They can learn about the event, register attendance, or put themselves down as a maybe. The manner and amount of interaction is determined by the creator of the event page. Event pages, like regular pages, turn up on the profiles of people who have registered an interest in the event as well as on the profile of the person who created the event. Events can be anything from a presidential election to a walk in the park or a special discount day on a website. Are you beginning to see the potential here?

## Start a page

These are web pages you can visit or create within the Facebook site. They, like any other web page, can be about almost anything.

When you find a page you like, you can click on a button to become a fan. You can also "share" a page with a friend to give them the opportunity to view and become a fan of the page. When you, or anyone else for that matter, are a fan of a page, the page's image appears fairly prominently on your profile page. This gives further visibility to the page when people are visiting their friends' profiles, as you do on Facebook. So where are all these pages? Click on the cool Facebook toolbar at the bottom-left part of the page and browse and create pages. Start building your fan base of targeted Facebook users.

## Social media conclusion

Social media is the easiest and fastest way to be with your customers, because you can use it like a contact with your store and do some promotions.

# Handling orders and checking payments

Any day now you're going to get an e-mail from PrestaShop saying you have a new order! When you have stopped dancing around the room, read on to learn about handling orders and much more.

## Creating order messages

As you will see shortly, you have the facility to quickly send messages via e-mail to your customers by accessing their order. Considering that many of the messages will be identical, wouldn't it be useful to write those messages in advance and then, with the click of a button, send the message of our choice? Well, you can do that.

# Time for action – creating messages

Here's how you can create order messages:

1. Hover over the **Orders** tab and click on the **Order Messages** subtab. Then click on the green **Add new** button.

2. We are presented with a nice, simple form asking for the name of our message and the actual message itself. I suggest creating a message called **Dispatch notification**. Type in a brief and friendly message informing the customer that their product has been dispatched. You might like to create multiple versions of this message, perhaps for orders with different delivery methods, or times, or some other reason specific to your business.

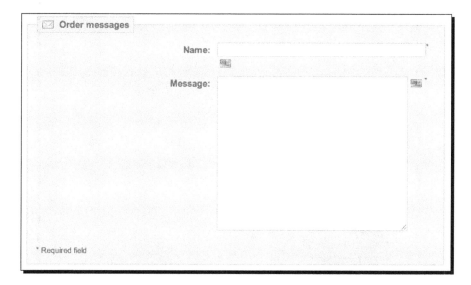

3. Save the message and then create as many messages as you think you will need. You can, of course, come back at any time to create a new message for a situation you didn't anticipate. You might like to create more messages like the dispatch notification, such as **Thanks for the cheque/bank wire**. Perhaps you have special orders or fluctuations in stock that require you to notify a customer when their order or part order has arrived? Note that the **Thanks for your order** messages are done automatically by PrestaShop.

## What just happened?

We have just composed some pre-prepared messages that we will use when processing customer orders. These can be great time savers; they help avoid a lot of typing. They also help us avoid errors and keep our customer contacts consistent.

## Statuses

Statuses keep our customers informed of the state of an order. They can view order statuses when they log in to their respective accounts. Statuses are very useful for managing our shop as well. PrestaShop creates a number of default statuses for us. These will probably suit the needs of most shops. The next *Time for action* section will introduce statuses.

## Time for action – statuses

Here we go.

1. Click on the **Statuses** subtab.

2. Take a look at all of the order statuses available to you by default.

3. Let's have a look at any one among them in detail. Click on the edit icon next to one of the statuses.

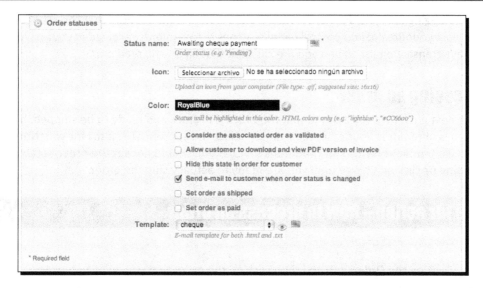

4. Here is an explanation. As you can see, I have selected the **Awaiting cheque payment** status. I could, if I wanted to, browse to find a graphic to represent that status. I can see that the highlighted color, when an order has this status, will be royal blue. The next four checkboxes give you options related to the customer. Probably the most interesting option is the **Template** option. This defines the e-mail template used to send a message to the customer when an order reaches this state.

5. Click on the little eye icon to view the e-mail that the customer would receive.

6. Go back to the list when you're done.

7. In the unlikely event that you do not have enough status options, click on **Add new** and you will see the same form we were just looking at. Fill it out to match the new status you are after.

## What just happened?

We looked at statuses and how to view at them in detail, including the message that a customer will receive. In the next two sections, we will actually make use of and change statuses as well as send some of the messages we created previously.

## Checking payments

Click on the **Orders** tab. If you had processed a sale from your willing volunteer, you will see the order there. Notice the **Paid** status in the **Status** column.

This is all well and good, but how can we be sure we have the money? It is always worth double checking whether a payment has actually arrived and has not been reversed or cancelled. Also, note that with Google Checkout, the customer's card is merely verified and is not actually charged until the order is processed.

I suggest logging into your PayPal or Google Checkout account to verify that the list of orders you have in your PrestaShop control panel matches the payments received in your payment provider's transaction list. When you are satisfied that all is well, read on.

# Processing an order

For this next guide, we will assume that the order is in stock and ready to be shipped. If the situation is different in your case, then simply select the appropriate status for you. Note that the Google Checkout terms and conditions say that you should not set the order's status to **Processing** or click on **Charge** until you are ready to actually ship the order.

## Time for action – how to process an order

Let's process our first order:

1. Click on the **Orders** tab and then click on the order that you want to process.

2. Click on the drop-down box and change the status of the order, as shown in the following screenshot. For example, if you are packing the order and about to go to the post office, select the **Shipped** status.

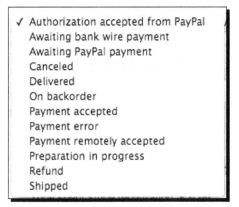

3. Scroll to the bottom of the order details page and click on the send message link, as highlighted in the following screenshot:

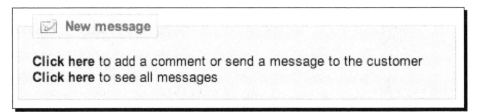

4. Select an appropriate default message to keep the customer up-to-date or to write a new message.

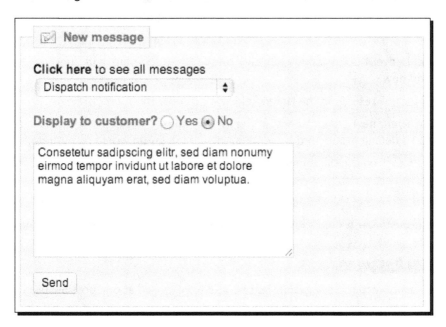

5. Wrap the customer's order, or do whatever you need to fulfill the order. Notice that there are two addresses, invoice and delivery. Often these are the same, but not always. If they are different, be sure to send to the delivery address.

## What just happened?

Now when you receive your first customer order, it can be a moment of joy and not one of panic.

Let's look in more detail at the **Customers** and **Orders** tabs to see some of your options.

# More about the Customers and Orders tabs

Here is a whirlwind tour of the **Customers** and **Orders** tabs, covering the most useful functions that have not been covered so far.

## Groups

Groups are potentially very useful. Not surprisingly, you can create groups and then add your customers to specific ones. The purpose is the interesting bit. You can then assign discounts to groups, and then all of the members of that group would qualify for that discount.

## Time for action – creating and using groups

Perhaps wholesale and retail could constitute a common group. Here we will create a group called **Wholesale**, give the group 10 percent discount, and then add some customers to it.

1. Hover over the **Customers** tab, click on the **Groups** subtab, and then click on **Add new**:

2. Enter Wholesale in the **Name** field and 10 in the **Discount (%)** field.

3. Save your new group. Notice, in the list of groups, there is the new wholesale group and a default group. In this scenario, the default group would be our retail group.

4. Now click on the **Customers** tab and then click on the edit icon on one of the customers.

5. Select the checkbox to add the customer to the wholesale group, then click on **Save**.

6. The customer will now enjoy any discounts assigned to the wholesale group.

## What just happened?

We now know how to use the groups feature and have looked at one possible use for it.

# Customers

You just saw how we edited the membership of a group via the **Customers** tab. You can also view a list of all the customers via this tab. Notice the empty boxes above each of the fields in the table of customers?

We can use the empty boxes to enter dates, names, partial names, and so on. Then we can click on the **Filter** button to see a new list of customers based on the filtering requirements we specified.

Also, try clicking on the magnify icon at the end of a customer's name and look at the full customer detail summary that pops up.

# Carts

The **Shopping Carts** tab under Customers is a very useful tool. We can see at a glance the carts that were created in our store and when they were created. Note that this tab is very distinct from **Orders**. Lots of carts being created that don't lead to orders could be an indication of a problem—perhaps something the customer didn't like that put them off, and it is probably worth investigating.

We can click on any of the carts and get an expanded description of it.

# Invoices

There are two main uses for invoices. First, our customers might want one, especially if they made a purchase for their businesses, and second, it is good practice to keep a copy for yourself for accounting purposes.

## Time for action – Invoices

Make sure that you are logged in to your admin control panel and then read on.

1. Hover over the **Orders** tab and then click on the **Invoices** subtab.

2. In the **Invoice options** panel shown in the preceding screenshot, select **Yes** to enable invoices for your customers.

3. In the **Invoice number** box, you can specify the number of the next invoice to be generated. This is a great cheat for hiding the fact that your shop is brand new. When your first ever customer gets the invoice number 5456753, they will have no idea how special they really are.

4. Look at the button labeled **Generate PDF file by date**.

5. Specify a date period, perhaps the beginning and the end of a particular month.

6. Click on the **Generate PDF file by date** button and you can easily print all of your customer invoices for that month.

## What just happened?

We saw how to enable and disable customer invoices as well as print invoices for our own records.

## Merchandise returns

Here you can enable merchandise returns as well as specify the number of days after ordering for which this is acceptable.

Once this is enabled, you can then assign return statuses on you orders screen. This includes **waiting for package**, **package received**, **refund given**, and **return denied**.

## Pop quiz – Sell your products

Q1. I have a new product and I absolutely must shout out about it *now*. Which one of these is an appropriate outlet?

1. Talk to my family and friends about my new business.

2. Forums, specialized websites, search engine registration, and AdWords.

3. Search engine registration and AdWords.

Q2. What kind of products and shops benefit from a customer loyalty program?

1. Products that the customer buys only once a year.

2. Products that the customer often buys.

3. Only rare items.

Q3. How else would you market your site for free?

1. By having a good SEO strategy, writing good posts, and giving good customer service.

2. By having a good customer service.

3. Using SEO is more than enough.

# Summary

Now you know everything you need to know to make money from your e-commerce business. Specifically:

◆ We created a customer account and used it to test the checkout process, write some product comments, and practice processing an order

◆ We set up a PrestaShop customer loyalty scheme

◆ We made sure that all of the major search engines know about your great new shop

◆ We looked at the beginning of social media marketing

◆ We looked at some extra functions of the **Customers** and **Orders** tabs that weren't covered by the rest of the chapter

The most important information, however, is in the next chapter. You will learn how to grow your new small business into a massive e-commerce empire. Find out the big secret to turning a successful small business into a massive one, and explore why you would even want to anyway. *Chapter 9, Go... to the Future* has all this and more.

# 9
# Go... to the Future

*Welcome to the last chapter. This is the chapter that can make the most difference to your new business. The really simple tools and ideas that we discuss here are the key to turning your nice little PrestaShop store into a thriving e-commerce empire.*

In this chapter, we shall look at:

◆ Why we do this

◆ Analyzing, optimizing, and adding

◆ The big secret

◆ The future of e-commerce and PrestaShop

So let's get on with it.

## Why are we here?

My science teacher used to boom this question across the classroom and scare half the class into paying attention. But it is a good question and well worth thinking about.

What is critical, especially in this type of business, is to understand what we are trying to achieve. This is necessary because a deep understanding and certainty of purpose will guide our actions. Although our PrestaShop store might be just about done, our business must have a real and clear purpose, and path, in order for us to achieve the maximum we can with our newfound knowledge.

So why did we open a PrestaShop store? Why did you buy this book? For some of you, it might be simple curiosity about PrestaShop or perhaps e-commerce in general. I am guessing that for the majority of us, it was to start a business. And for any number of good reasons, you specifically chose PrestaShop.

But why did you want to start a business at all? Well, that's obvious you might say—to make money. But why make money? To pay the bills. It is probably obvious what I am hinting at. You may think here that there is some impending lecture on home-work balance—I promise you, there won't be.

However, I hope you have considered exactly what you would like to provide for yourself and your family through this business. In particular, are you doing this for the thrill of an online business? That's fine, I am. Or are you just looking at an online business to provide you with the means to give yourself and your family what you deserve? That's fine as well, me too.

I just wanted to point out one or two things that might not be immediately obvious.

# The power of e-commerce and a passive income

You have, at this stage, an opportunity for a little bit more than just paying the bills. I am not suggesting that we should, all or any of us, try and be extremely wealthy entrepreneurs. There isn't anything wrong with that, though. I am not suggesting we should, all or any of us, be big business people and dominate our markets, although that is OK as well.

I am not even suggesting that we should consider e-commerce, PrestaShop, or any other e-business tool to be anything more important than just that, a mere tool. But it would be negligent of me, having strung you along for more than 200 pages, not to double check whether you fully realized the power and potential of what you just started.

## The busy billionaire

I admire people who work hard. And to have a successful e-commerce business, you have to work very hard indeed. But unlike a high-powered job or conventional self-employment, a self-built e-commerce website offers the opportunity for income without the massive time constraints and life-dominating commitment required by most other businesses and by every form of employment.

I am not trying to describe an income that is necessarily big, although it can be, but an income that you control and not one that controls you.

The rest of this chapter will go on to explain how to use PrestaShop in conjunction with other tools to grow your income, but with only a very minimal time commitment. Starting a business like this should not be the precursor to a full-time job. In fact, just the opposite can be true.

What I am trying to get to is this: PrestaShop, when used efficiently, can be the start of a significant passive income. That is, an income that keeps coming in, even when you are not actually working on it. Don't believe me? Read on.

# Learning from competitors

If there is something that our competitors have, it is their level of learning. We could have the best e-commerce site in the world but we need to keep an eye on our competitors, because your customers will be doing exactly that.

On the Internet, it is very easy to check different stores in few minutes; you need to give something more to your customers. This could be very good customer service, an amazing design, price, items, and so on; they could all help keep the customers in your store. For that, you need to learn from your competitors; maybe they have the key, and you can learn it and improve it.

# Perpetual analysis, improvement, and marketing

The key theme here is in the word perpetual, which means continuing without interruption. Marketing, optimizing, and improving your website is not a one-off job. It has to be done on an ongoing basis—it is never finished. That's the bad news. The good news is that it doesn't have to take long, just so long as it is done on a regular basis. And as your website becomes more established, I would suggest that the amount of time you spend on optimization be decreased, as long as the frequency is maintained. This is good news and sits well with our plan for a passive income.

First of all, let's look at how we can measure the performance of our PrestaShop site.

## Analyzing statistics

In *Chapter 5, Tools, Newsletters, Extra Income, and Statistics*, we set up the PrestaShop statistics modules as well as installed Google Analytics. Now we will look at how you can use them to understand some areas for change and improvement in your PrestaShop store. It is also worth pointing out that, quite often, the statistics gathered by Analytics will overlap with what have been gathered by PrestaShop. However, as we will see, both do have unique statistics that the other doesn't. First of all, we will look at the built-in PrestaShop features.

# PrestaShop statistics

Look at the huge menu of stats options in the next screenshot. We very briefly looked at them in *Chapter 5, Tools, Newsletters, Extra Income, and Statistics*. Here we will try and deduce how to use them in a practical way. Try and glean useful information that can then be used to make changes and improve our stores. You can access the menu by clicking on the **Stats** tab. The menu is located toward the bottom, on the left-hand side of the page.

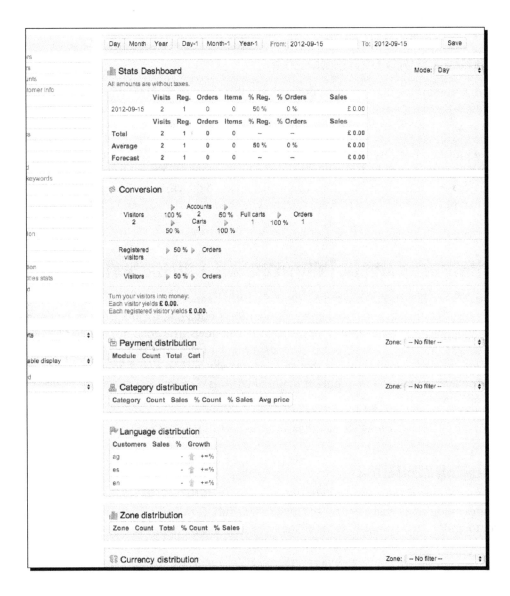

The actual statistics themselves are very straightforward, but sometimes their meaning is less obvious. We will cover the most common, useful stats, but what is useful to one business might not be to another. Be sure to think about all of the information PrestaShop gathers for you and how you might be able to use it.

## Pages not found

First up is **Pages not found**. This happens when a visitor tries to visit a page on our site that doesn't exist. This statistic then records the details of pages that visitors tried to visit that don't exist and how often it happened.

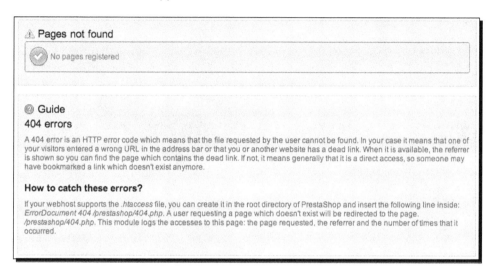

What you are aiming for is to get the message shown in the screenshot shown just previously. **No pages registered** means there were no pages that couldn't be found. If you have one or more pages not found, it is probably a really good idea to find out why and fix this.

A common cause of pages not found is broken links (that is, you have made a link on your site and mistyped the URL). Perhaps you created a link in an article to `./teddybearf` when it should have been `./teddybears`. This would cause an entry to be created in the **Pages not found** statistics. Another cause for this is where the page was real but was, for some reason, removed. Then when visitors click on links to the page, which should otherwise not have been removed, you will get the details of this here.

When a customer comes across a broken link, it is highly likely that they will give up on your site. So check the **Pages not found** statistics regularly and fix or remove links that cause problems.

## Best products, best categories, and catalog statistics

These three statistics pages can be used in conjunction with one another. Why not go and have a look at the **Best products**, **Best categories**, and **Catalog statistics** now. The **Catalog statistics** category has been shown in the following screenshot:

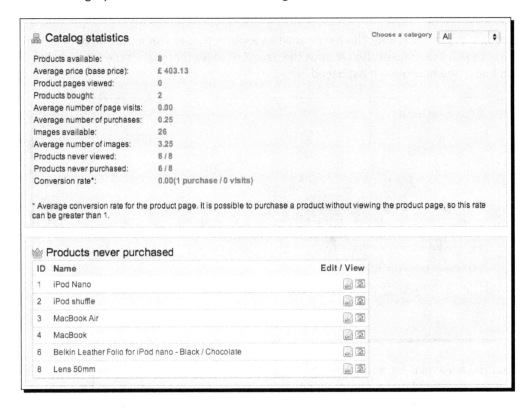

On the **Best products** page, there is a wealth of information. See the following screenshot:

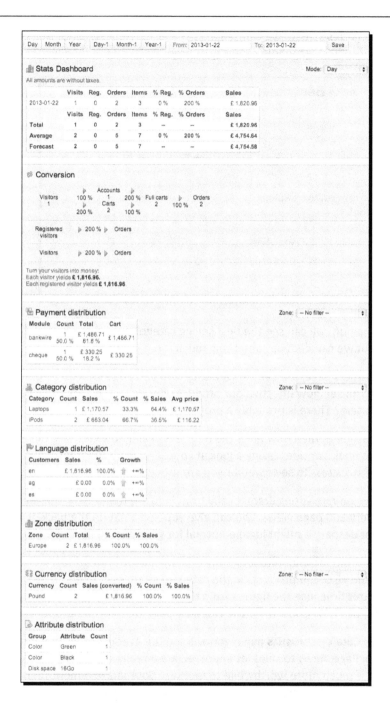

On the **Best categories** screen, we can see a narrower range of statistics that tell us about a broader range of subjects (a whole category of products). See the following screenshot:

| Best categories | | | |
|---|---|---|---|
| **Name** ▲▼ | **Total Quantity Sold** ▲▼ | **Total Price Sold** ▲▼ | **Total Viewed** ▲▼ |
| Root > Home | 8 | 1833.61 | 0 |
| Home > Laptops | 1 | 1170.57 | 0 |
| Home > iPods | 7 | 663.04 | 0 |
| Home > Cameras | 0 | 0.00 | 0 |
| Home > Accessories | 0 | 0.00 | 0 |
| **Displaying 1 - 5 of 5** | | | |

From this information, we can see the best selling categories and products, which of course is interesting, but we can deduce something much more useful as well.

On the **Best products** page, look at the **Quantity sold** and **Page viewed** columns. From these two figures, we can see how effective our product offering is. Have you received 150-page views without a sale? There is probably a problem.

Is the price good? If it is, then how full is the description and how clear are the images? If you pass the last two tests, consider taking a look at your sales copy and referring to *Chapter 3, Merchandising for Success* to see whether you are using the best possible sales copy.

A "good" conversion rate varies dramatically from industry to industry, but if you are getting five sales for every 100 page views, you can give yourself a pat on the back. If yours is lower than this, do not despair, it might just be normal for your type of product.

You can use the same technique to judge the effectiveness of categories, including the category page and all of the products in the category combined. Use exactly the same technique, but this time, use the figures from the best category page. You will often find the number of sales per view is lower for the category page than for the product page.

Now look at the **Catalog statistics** page; you will see the average sales and page views across the whole store. Page views to sales, at any level, are a really good benchmark to measure your success. It is much more worthwhile to measure your improvement than to try and compare with somebody else's figures (or even the figures I just gave). The figures I gave are just a very rough guide.

If you think you could improve, we will look at a plan for continuous improvement in a bit.

## Shop search

This page is simple. It shows you the search terms being used in your search box. This is obviously distinct from the search terms being used on the search engines; we will come to them when we look at Google Analytics.

The terms that people use to search your shop can tell you many things. For example, if people are searching extensively for a particular term or two, it means that they are finding your site easily, but perhaps the specific item or article they are looking for is proving to be more elusive.

Visit your shop front and try out the search term. Does it take you to the page you expected? If not, you probably need to look at your meta tags and search weightings (discussed in *Chapter 4, Getting More Customers*). If it does give you the expected page, great! But that is not necessarily the end of the matter. If people are using a search term a lot, is it worth making the thing easier to find? You could perhaps feature it on the home page, have it added to your tag cloud, or make the category more prominent by moving it up the category list order. Not all these things should definitely be done, but should at least be considered. Don't rush off and do it now. Make a note, and we will look at when to schedule such tasks soon.

## PrestaShop statistics summary

The statistics features that are useful to you will not be the same as those that are useful to everybody else. Try and get familiar with all of them and then apply your knowledge of your industry to make them useful to you.

# Google Analytics

Log in to your Analytics account and look at the huge menu of Analytics options. Here we will try and deduce how to make use of them. Try and glean useful meaning from the data, which can then be used to make changes and improve our stores.

Like Google AdWords (more soon), Analytics is a massive topic. I will cover perhaps the most useful features here. However, if you find that using these features is getting results, then I would definitely recommend further study. For example, you can link Analytics to AdWords to fully explore how viable your AdWords are. But that goes beyond the space we have here. Let's get on with it.

## Audience

The following screenshot shows the number of daily visitors to a website. This is interesting, and of course, we should strive to increase it. This screenshot only displays the number of daily visitors for a month. However, you use the buttons at the top-right corner to change the date range to whatever you like.

If you are a brand new store, a short date range can be very telling. If you have been open for a while, extend the overall date range, and look for a steady upward increase.

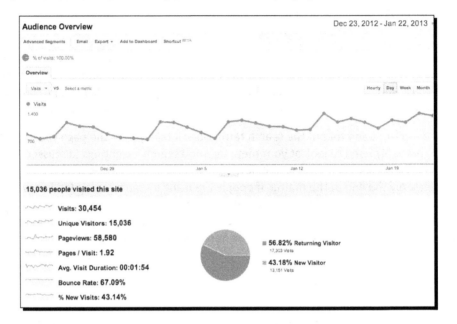

Log in to Analytics, select your site, and click on **Audience**. We will discuss some of the mines of precious information that you can dig up on the **Audience** tab.

You have options like new versus returning. This tells us how many of our visitors are repeat customers and how many are new. The actual figures are imperfect because the technology is also imperfect at detecting return visitors. But it is a very good guide.

Not enough return visitors? You need to give people a reason to come back to your store. Perhaps the customer loyalty scheme discussed in *Chapter 8, Ready to Sell* can help, or a discount voucher may be sent out to existing customers. If there aren't enough new visitors, you need to employ all the marketing tools that you can. Have a look at the following screenshot; it compares new and returning visitors:

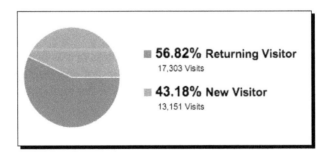

You can also click on **Frequency & Recency** to see a full breakdown of the number of customers who visited once or more than once.

**Engagement** is a great indicator of how long people stayed, and describes this in great detail. It shows how many stayed for 0 to 10 seconds, 11 to 30 seconds, and so on. Your aim is to get people to browse your site for as long as possible. If you are getting a high percentage of your visitors who leave in under 30 seconds, look into the pages (in detail) that they are viewing (and not liking). Then try and work out why, and fix it.

Have a look at your map overlay. It allows you to hover your mouse pointer over different regions of the world and see where your visitors live. If you're getting lots of visitors from countries you don't ship to or from countries that speak languages you don't cater for, it might be time for a rethink.

The options under **Audience** are immense, and exploring them is highly recommended. We will soon look at how to best spend time searching for and using statistics.

## Traffic sources

Traffic sources refers to the manner in which our visitors arrived at our site, as opposed to the geographical location talked about earlier. The options are: links from other sites, the different search engines, and people typing in a URL or clicking on a bookmark.

If you don't have many referrals from other websites, you need to start marketing your site on forums, blogs, and social media. If you find that any of the major search engines are missing your site completely, then you need to check whether you registered. Go back and check *Chapter 8, Ready to Sell*.

Under **Traffic Sources Overview**, you can click on keywords and see mountains of information about the keywords that made search engines send visitors to your site. This can be very revealing. Are they what you expected? Do you need to refine your search engine optimization discussed in *Chapter 4, Getting More Customers* or do you need to start writing articles and creating product categories or product descriptions for a whole new set of keywords? Think about it, but don't rush off and do anything major until you have read the rest of this chapter.

## Content

Content, as the title suggests, gets down to the specifics of each page. The simplest use of content statistics is to determine how many entrances to your site came from each page. See which pages had the most views overall. These are the ones that must be made as perfect as possible. That is, you can use the best sales copy, the best images, or if it's an article, make sure it is linked to the appropriate product pages. However, don't change too much; the page could lose its popularity if you change too many keyword attributes.

### Google Analytics summary

As with the PrestaShop statistics, the Analytics features that are useful to you will not be the same as those that are useful to somebody else. Try and get familiar with all of them and then apply knowledge of your industry to make them useful to you.

# Improvement

Hopefully, the discussion on statistics will enable you to identify potential areas for change. But perhaps most of the enhancing and updating will be done based on your knowledge of your industry or how it is changing. For examples, read on.

## Optimizing your articles, product descriptions, and category descriptions

You should constantly be updating your articles to keep them current. If something changes in your industry, and that affects something in one of your articles, change the article. You might be surprised at how quickly the search engines pick up on it. Thought of a better way to describe a product? Then update that too. Can you improve your grammar in any way? Can you use your statistics to change or optimize the density of the actual keywords that you use? Did you find a new great image to use somewhere on your site? Constantly updating and amending your content keeps it fresh and scores big marks with search engines and humans.

### Adding new articles

Keep looking out for new topics to write articles about. Once your articles have been indexed by the search engines, you might be amazed at how responsive they are. I have added new articles and found them in search results just hours later. And this can be true for sites with fairly modest profiles.

So if there is something important, topical, or controversial in your industry, write about it and make sure it is linked with other relevant articles on your site. Having said what I have, don't write articles for the sake of it. If it is not genuinely relevant, don't bother. If a once-relevant article has become irrelevant, take it down. It is not a competition about quantity but quality and relevance.

# Marketing

We have already talked about many different forms of marketing. The main point to make here is that these forms of marketing should also be perpetual. If you log in to your industry forum once every six months and post a hundred messages, you will be judged as a self-promoter and there will be no benefit to your business. If, however, you post a small number of relevant messages or replies once a week across all the platforms, you will reap enormous benefits over time.

It is the same with e-mail marketing your site. If you send an e-mail a day for a week, your subscribers will be reaching for the spam button. However, sending one well-constructed newsletter per month (or whatever frequency is right for you) will bring new customers and repeat customers.

You know how to make changes to your AdWords campaign. This too is best looked at on a perpetual basis, at a frequency relevant to your specific business. So if you are getting 60 percent of all your sales via AdWords, then you should look at it with a higher frequency than for when you have a small spend with small returns.

## Devising a routine and sticking to it

Think about all the things we have talked about. You could make some notes and then read on.

## Time for action – making a plan

This quick guide will help you create a monthly plan for perpetual improvement of your website. The key is to be as efficient as possible and take up as little time as possible, but at the same time, making sure that nothing is being neglected.

1. Write down a list of all the different marketing activities you are involved in and, next to that, the frequency with which you think you should be doing them. Next to that, also write the amount of time (in hours) you think it will take.

2. Write down a list of all the optimization activities that you expect to engage in, and (like you did in the previous point) the frequency and expected time you will take for each activity.

3. Now do exactly the same as the previous step, but this time, as an estimate for adding new content. This includes articles, categories, and products.

4. Now estimate the amount of time that you will set aside for customer service and the handling of orders (which you will probably be doing quite frequently).

5. Now using that information, write out a monthly plan showing the days divided into one-hour slots so that you can see the spare time that you have.

6. Your final plan should show a very small amount of time, perhaps for each day (for me it is an hour per day), for customer service and packing. You will probably have a frequently recurring block. For me, it is half a day per week that I spend on marketing, optimizing, and adding. The vast majority of your monthly planner will hopefully, at least for now, be empty.

## What just happened?

The result should show vast empty spaces, to be spent as you please. If you have achieved your financial objectives, this time could be spent just doing what you please. If, like me, you have not achieved this yet, you could spend the spare time working on new projects. More on this soon.

It is worth mentioning that while writing this book, I spent no more than a few hours a week across all my stores. But my income went up! The amount of time you spend developing your PrestaShop store is not that important, but what matters is what you actually do with the time.

Now that we have the management of our websites down to a tee, we can look at what we would like to do with all our newly-found spare time.

# The big secret

So you have a working e-commerce business and you know how to develop and increase profitability. We have also discussed how to do this with the smallest time commitment possible. Starting an e-commerce business should not be about becoming a full-time, online equivalent of a shelf stacker, checkout operator, and store manager, all rolled into one. It is about getting technology to go to work for you.

There comes a time when any business begins to reach its full potential, and it is just as important to know that the development and improvement cycle we discussed earlier takes time, perhaps years. What if you are not making all you want from your store yet? What if you have successfully replaced whatever income you previously had, but you now have a taste of success and you want more? What should you do?

Just do what every successful business has always done. But first, a bit about conventional business.

## High street retail

Walk down any shopping street or any modern shopping mall in almost any town or city around the world and you are faced with a wall of recognizable brands. McDonalds is an obvious example.

In 1954, a milkshake machine salesman called Ray Kroc was fascinated by why one particular hamburger restaurant in California, USA was so much more successful than any of his other customers' restaurants. There were a number of elements that made the McDonald brothers' restaurant better than the others, but that is not the point of the story.

Ray Kroc made a deal with the McDonald brothers and started opening more burger restaurants using their successful formula. Every new restaurant brought a significant increase in sales, but without the initial risk and time commitment of the first. Why? It had been done before, he knew it worked, and he knew (from experience) how to get up and running very quickly and avoid all of the pitfalls. Ten years later, there were 700 McDonalds restaurants.

So how does this help us? You have reached this point, so you already know how to open an e-commerce business. You know how to run it without a significant investment in time. So what are you going to do next? I struggled to open my first e-commerce store. It took months, and it looked awful, and I mean it when I say awful. But guess what? It worked because I used open source software that had already been tried and tested by thousands of other businesses, and people purchased my stuff. Not much initially, but in time.

So I opened another. This time it was a bit smarter-looking, took only a few weeks, and was a little bit more successful. Can you guess what I did next? Yes, I opened another one and it was even easier than the last one. And I didn't stop there.

For those of you who have completed my 7-day challenge, congratulations! For those of you who took a bit longer, much longer, or are still waiting for your first customer, don't worry about it; keep going. Keep refining your PrestaShop and don't wait for it to be a hit before you open another one.

# Duplication

The technical term for copying a successful business over and over is duplication. Think about McDonalds again for a moment. Why did it work for them? Two important factors were that first, people liked it, and second, when people went to another town or city, they saw the golden arches and recognized it as a brand they liked. This, of course, is how all of the big names on the high street succeed, with duplication—brand awareness. And brand awareness is where my suggested model of duplication is completely different from that of the high street.

If you walk through a mall, you see all the usual suspects. Go and take a look at their online presence. They usually only have one main web store. Why? Simple, because as we talked about just now, people are drawn in by brand awareness. For the high street or a shopping mall, they are drawn in by location and brand awareness. On the Internet, having five Circuit City computer store websites won't work. They are only successful because the name and perhaps the domain name are very well-known.

This can't help us because we don't want to spend loads of money building brand awareness. So how are we going to duplicate our business?

## Look at it like this

When I was a very young boy, I used to love going to the local corner shop to buy a quarter of Cola Cubes. Sometimes, I would be sent on a short errand to get a loaf of bread or a pint of milk. Other times, we would all go in the car and get a whole load of things because we didn't have time to go to the supermarket that week. That little corner shop was a busy, bustling, and thriving business. It was a part of our local community, and a big part of my small world back then.

As I got a little older and travelled further afield, I noticed that there were other corner shops. Not always on actual corners, but the same type of thing. They would all specialize in something slightly different, but still have a core range of everyday products. There was one that had a great range of toys, another had books, another had baked goods, and so on.

And eventually, I realized that these places existed in the thousands all over the UK. And those similar businesses existed in the millions across every continent in the world. The point is that they were all successful businesses in their own right. How did they all succeed, so close to one another? Perhaps the obvious answer is that they all served their own specific community, defined approximately by distance from the next corner shop.

## An analogy to explain

It is true that the independently owned, small-store business is in something of a decline, at least in the UK anyway. But only because the big companies are buying them or replacing them, not because that type of business has no demand. Big companies can use their financial might to monopolize this market just as they did for the high street, malls, and out-of-town sites. It is hard, if not impossible, to compete.

But on the Web, the rules are very different and the advantage, I believe, is with the small business. Here is why. Tesco has the largest share of the UK supermarket business with hundreds of stores around the country. They also have an incredibly successful online presence through `www.tesco.com`, which delivers the customers' shopping to their homes. So if it is so successful, why don't they open another website that does the same thing and multiply their business? Perhaps `www.tesco-two.com`. I checked, the name is available. Simply because all that would happen is that if the site was successful, it would only get business from the existing site, `www.tesco.com`. There would be no new customers because Tesco's online business, like the other big names, is entirely dependent on their brand awareness. Herein lies the first major difference between our duplication model and theirs.

When we create another store, it must be different from the last—with a new domain name, new product and category descriptions, perhaps a slightly varied range, and perhaps even new prices. By creating an apparently unique business, we are potentially doubling our income. Why does this work for us but not for Tesco or other big businesses?

I am well aware that at this point I have created more questions than I have answered. This works for us and not the big boys because we do it ourselves in a fraction of the time and at a microscopic percentage of the cost to them. With their unwieldy, inflexible size, they cannot specialize in niches. They would need designers, buyers, marketing, staff, managers, and the list goes on. We need a spare day or two and $5 a month for hosting, if that is the case.

The returns on such an investment would be too slow for a shareholder-owned organization. And the one thing that the big boys will never have, which is essential to make a success of this type of business, is a person with the passion for the products and a commitment to its success. Money can never buy this.

## What about all these corner shops?

So why did I go on about the corner shops? What have they got to do with it? Simple; think about search engine optimization for a minute. It is a bit unclear, to say the least. What keywords to use, what density, page structure, formatting, whether to use meta tags or not! It makes my head spin.

Big organizations and others that have only one main website have to get it right—exactly right, or their business will fail. They have to spend fortunes researching keywords, buying Google AdWords, paying affiliates, and the list goes on. Most of these tasks rely on employing expensive outside agencies or in-house "experts" because they have no choice but to get it right. And guess what happens when Google or another one of the search engines changes its ranking formula? They start again on an endless frantic circle of trying to convince the search engines that they should be at the top.

Yes, we must optimize and refine, as discussed earlier. However, if we have a dozen stores all feeding off of slightly different keywords and phrases, all with their own slightly different structure, formatting, and density, then any change in the search engine ranking formula is just as likely to benefit some of our stores as it is to be detrimental to others. We win. Oh yes, the corner shops.

Our websites are just like the corner shops. They are small, well-run, highly efficient, have zero unnecessary expenses, and make a modest income (each) by offering genuine products and services, preferably to repeat customers.

Where the analogy most applies with corner shops is, by making each site unique, we end up placing ourselves on lots of different virtual corners created by the vagaries of the search engines. If I have a laptop shop, do I optimize for laptops, notebooks, netbooks, or portable PCs? It doesn't matter all that much because I can optimize for them all, placing myself on as many virtual corners as I like.

These days, when people search for my products, I am confident that no matter what they call them, one of my sites will appear in the organic search results. The money, when they buy something, all goes to the same place.

The corner shop analogy stops working when we have only a tiny financial investment per store, almost zero time commitment once it is up and running, and an ongoing residual income for the foreseeable future! So let's get duplicating.

# Technical duplication tips

So we know that our stores must be different because we are not aiming for success through brand awareness, although you might surprise yourself and end up with one or more of your sites becoming well-known, but that is not our specific goal here.

## Varying your payment provider

Let's say you have a dozen thriving stores, you and your family are starting to live the life you deserve and all of a sudden, for no apparent reason, PayPal suspends your account. Hero to zero, and there is probably nothing you can do about it. Even if there is, it will almost certainly take time to get to the bottom of what got PayPal into a tizzy. And please believe me, they do get into a tizzy from time to time.

When you do your second PrestaShop site, why not choose an alternative payment provider? There are others, as well as the few options we looked at earlier. Visit www.prestastore.com and www.presto-changeo.com to see the list of payment modules available for PrestaShop.

Once you have a few stores up and running with different payment methods, consider installing two or more options in each store. Then, if a payment provider becomes unusable for any reason, you can simply disable the unwanted one and enable another. You can also consider having more than one enabled at the same time to give your customers a choice.

## Varying your web host

Problems can arise with web hosts. Problems such as downtime can occur, they can get hacked, and so on. Keeping all of your websites on one host could be catastrophic. It is certainly okay to have a few per host, otherwise our web-hosting bill would quickly go through the roof, but don't keep too many for each.

The other good reason to vary your web host is that in a shared hosting environment, the IP address that identifies your web server could be the same for all sites. This could potentially cause issues with the search engines, which might object to too many related sites being on the same IP address.

## Varying your content

This is crucial. You can save time by using your old content as a template and also perhaps using some of the same images, but your category, product, and article pages must be unique or the site will not perform in search engine rankings, because it might be considered as duplicate content.

Also, like the corner shops, vary your products. Once you are making a profit, which should be almost straight away, consider adding new products or even whole ranges. Vary the products and ranges that you put into different stores. After a year or two, it will start becoming apparent as to which store is going to be your top performer; you can use this as your main store to try out new things and then move successful products into different stores.

## Varying your cart software

PrestaShop is arguably the best. But there are loads, and I mean loads, of alternatives. The truth is that depending upon the criteria you use to judge the software, different products come out best. For example, if you are getting lots of visitors from your articles, and there are lots more that you could write, you definitely need to consider an open source solution where the focus is on the CMS, but with a shop attached. Check out `www.wordpress.org`, and get a great book on the subject from `www.packtpub.com`.

If you want to stick with the traditional e-commerce model but want to vary your structure and formatting (at the same time as getting your teeth into a new open source software title with different advantages and features), then go and have a look at `www.zen-cart.com`, `www.oscommerce.net`, or `www.magentocommerce.com`.

Also consider some quick and simple regular HTML websites. Make yourself a really simple three or four-page website. Use the template of your choice for free, from `www.oswd.org`, and put on some simple **buy now** buttons, which you can create in your Google Checkout or PayPal account.

## Try something totally new

I always wanted to have my own business but I never wanted one of the traditional forms of self-employment. I wanted to do something a bit different. The problem is, I am risk averse. It never ceases to amaze me the courage shown by some entrepreneurs while financing their new ventures: huge loans, re-mortgages, and so on.

The problem with this type of venture, of course, is that there are consequences if the business is not a success. I am, for this reason, a sort of do-it-yourself e-commerce kind of person. If a business fails, then I have lost some time, not my shirt, and if during that time I was earning money from other businesses, then it is not too much of a problem. As your experience of different software solutions grows, something happens inside your brain. Let me explain.

You begin to realize just how vast and varied the world of open source is. Just about anything can be achieved on the Web, for nothing or almost nothing when you do it yourself, and you would be surprised how simple some of the things actually are, when you thought they would be really hard.

As this world of possibilities dawns on you, if it hasn't already, you might find, all of a sudden that your ideas have become much more varied and adventurous. For example, I found myself dabbling in the likes of education websites, product comparisons, and business services as well as good old e-commerce.

Once you have a virtually passive income and just a little knowledge in a lot of fields, you will find that ideas for new websites come faster than you can possibly use them. Why not diversify totally? Think through these marvelous possibilities, plan how realistic they are, and dive into your favorite. I have found, without exception, that there is always the opportunity for cross-promotion with your existing businesses.

And if the fluffy teddy or bikes business falls a bit flat for a year or two, your diversification will make your income more resilient. If you see yourself as an entrepreneur, I recommend investigating a few technologies. You do not need to master any of them, just understand the basics and how to use the hard work done by others to your advantage. If this is you, read about HTML, CSS, jQuery, PHP, and MySQL writing for the Web and web development in general. You can get beginner's books on many of these topics from www.packtpub.com.

# The future of e-commerce and PrestaShop

So you want to know what will be the next big thing. Well this is it. Are you ready?

We can only guess the changes that will occur in the world of e-commerce. New customer trends will surely come and go; new features that we can only imagine will appear in shopping cart software. For example, in the short time that elapsed while writing this book, PrestaShop went through two versions and had multiple upgrades.

As we have discussed at length, your first PrestaShop store is only the beginning. The possibilities are only restricted by our imaginations. All you need to decide is what part you are going to play. Keeping abreast of new developments in technology is the key to taking advantage of all the possibilities that future opportunities present. In the appendix, there is a list of online resources. Why not visit them all and join any forums that look interesting. Introduce yourself, watch the conversations that interest you, and join in the discussion when you can. You will quickly have your finger on the pulse of e-business.

## Pop quiz – become an e-commerce expert

Q1. Why is creating brand awareness not necessarily the best policy for expanding our e-commerce business?

1. It is more important to have a very good product line and customer services.
2. It is better to have good marketing and invest in AdWords.
3. The most important thing is to create brand awareness.

Q2. Can you find out, by searching the Web, what the top three open source shopping cart software are?

1. Magento, PrestaShop, and osCommerce.
2. PrestaShop, Shopify, and CubeCart.
3. OpenCart, Axis Commerce, and PrestaShop.

Q3. In Google Analytics, which main options help us identify areas where improvement/optimization might help and which main option helps us prioritize those improvements?

1. Real-time.
2. Audience.
3. Traffic Sources.

# Picture this

It's 6 o'clock on Monday morning. You are not really looking forward to another grueling week at work. Another five days of office politics. Another small chunk of your life dedicated to making somebody else rich—giving somebody else's family the finer things in life, while somebody else decides what you are worth by the hour!

And then you remember you don't do that anymore. You started your own online business about six months ago and handed in your notice last Friday. You go downstairs and make a coffee. It smells good. You sit in your favorite chair and switch on your laptop. You check your e-mails.

You see you have made some more sales overnight. You log in to your PrestaShop control panel and all of the payments have been confirmed. You process the orders. You check the news headlines as you sip your coffee. You shut down your laptop. You ponder your next big idea. The day is your own while PrestaShop works slavishly. What will you do and where will you go?

# Summary

Well, that's just about it. This chapter covered:

- The point of running our own e-business in the first place
- How to develop your business in an ongoing manner
- The big secret to multiplying your business income in whichever way you want
- The future of business on the Internet—it's hard to predict but with a bit of effort, simple to keep up with

I wish you every success with your PrestaShop business and please let me know how you get on via www.tizonsoft.net/en/contact. Much more than this, I hope you take advantage of the huge opportunity presented to us all through open source projects like PrestaShop.

In a world becoming more and more dominated by giant institutions that can sometimes seek to control how much we earn and the type of lives that we lead, we can use the world of open source to take back what should be ours and find ourselves much better placed to provide for our families and serve our communities.

# Control Panel Quick Reference

*What follows here is a really a brief account of every tab and subtab.
While we have already covered the tabs, I will remind you in which chapter(s)
this occurred.*

## Catalog

On the **Catalog** tab you can quickly create, edit, and delete categories and products. Here is what you will find on the subtabs:

## Products

Here you can list, edit, add, and delete new products in your store.

## Categories

In this subcategory, you can separate your products into different groups.

## Monitoring

This is a summary of your shop categories including empty categories, disabled, and out-of-stock products.

## Attributes and Values

This is a very powerful feature that enables you define product attributes, group them, and then assign them to products. This can be a big timesaver as well as really useful to your catalog and your customers.

## Features

This is a great way to add a list of product features to a separate tab underneath the main product description. This is a good place to put all the information a customer might want to know without cluttering the main product description. See *Chapter 3, Merchandising for Success*.

## Suppliers

You can enter the names and extra information about your suppliers. There are a number of good reasons for doing this. If your supplier is a trade secret then this one is not for you.

## Image Mapping

This is cool. Assign multiple clickable zones to an image so that different product pages can be opened by a single image. Go and have a look on the **Image Mapping** subtab. A full guide is given there.

## Tags

Create tags for any or all of your products, and assign different tags for each language.

## Attachments

This is potentially very useful. Here is an example. On the **Attachments** tab click on **Add new** attachment. An attachment is a file, perhaps an image or a PDF file. Then on your product creation page you can click on its attachment tab and add as many attachments as you like. Now on the products page that the customer sees, there will be a downloads tab. This is great for technical documents, instructions, large images, or anything else you might want the customer to have access to but do not want to actually put in the product description.

# Orders

Quickly see and sort all the orders you have received. Click on an order to process it. Order processing is covered in *Chapter 8, Ready to Sell*. Here is what you can do on the **Orders** subtabs:

| Subtab | Description |
|---|---|
| Invoices | There are two main uses for invoices. First, our customers might want one, especially if they made a purchase for their business, and second, it is a good practice to keep a copy for yourself for your accounting purposes. There's more in *Chapter 8, Ready to Sell*. |
| Merchandise Returns | Here you can enable merchandise returns as well as specify the number of days after order that this is acceptable. There's more in *Chapter 8, Ready to Sell*. |
| Delivery Slips | Print and configure delivery slips. |
| Credit Slips | View all your issued credit slips. |
| Statuses | What is the status of an order. Statuses tell us and the PrestaShop software what is occurring with any order. Assign, change, or create your own statuses. Have a read on *Chapter 8, Ready to Sell*. |
| Order Messages | Here you can add and amend customer messages. This is useful for sending messages that need to be sent many times. *Chapter 8, Ready to Sell*, looks at how to create and send messages. |

# Customers

Here you will find a list of customers. Click on one to view or edit the details. Here is a summary of all the subtabs under the **Customers** tab:

| Subtabs | Description |
|---|---|
| Addresses | View and edit all of your customer names and addresses at a glance or a click. |
| Groups | View, add, and edit customer groups. Customer groups can be used to assign discounts to some customers. Full details are provided in *Chapter 8, Ready to Sell*. |
| Shopping Carts | Use this tab in conjunction with your statistics. See the carts that customers fill and if they made a purchase. |
| Customer Service | Ticket system to resolve an issue or a question about our store. |
| Contacts | Here we will add our e-mail and description of every profile that could be in contact with us. |
| Titles | In this subtab will add all the titles that a customer can have. |

# Price Rules

It is the place to create discounts and vouchers.

## Cart Rules

Here you can create new vouchers.

## Catalog Price Rules

You can list, edit, add, or delete discount to your products.

# Shipping

Shipping has the potential to be the most complicated PrestaShop topic. But careful planning and implementation can keep things nice and simple. See *Chapter 7, Checkouts and Shipping* for full details. Read the following pages for a summary of the **Shipping** subtabs:

| Subtabs | Description |
| --- | --- |
| **Carriers** | Add and configure the carrier options to be used by your customers. Read *Chapter 7, Checkouts and Shipping* for all the ins and outs. |
| **Price Ranges** | This is one of the key, fundamental methods of shipping price configuration. Read more in *Chapter 7, Checkouts and Shipping*. |
| **Weight Ranges** | The other key, fundamental methods of shipping price configuration. Read more in *Chapter 7, Checkouts and Shipping*. |

# Localization

Localization has the potential to configure the units used for your products. The following subtabs are included under **Localization** tab:

| Subtabs | Description |
| --- | --- |
| Languages | Enable or disable all your languages that you want in your shop. |
| Zones | Add, remove, and configure the zones that you ship to. |
| Countries | Add, remove, and configure the countries that you ship to. |
| States | Add, remove, and configure the states that you ship to. |

| Subtabs | Description |
|---|---|
| Currencies | Add, configure, update, and delete the currencies used in your PrestaShop. *Chapter 7, Checkouts and Shipping*, goes into lots of detail about this, including auto updating currency exchange rates. |
| Taxes | Select, add, and configure the different tax rates that you need. *Chapter 7, Checkouts and Shipping*, gives you full reference on this. |
| Tax Rules | If you sell to different countries maybe you will need to set up different tax rules for every country. |
| Translations | Here you can modify translations for all text input in PrestaShop. |

# Modules

Just about anything you want to add to your store is done from here. Modules are mentioned, installed, and configured in just about every chapter.

## Modules & Themes Catalog

Search for new modules and themes from your store directly into the official PrestaShop repository.

## Positions

You can increase and decrease the priority of any module. If a module is at the highest priority (top of the list) it will be displayed first, within that position. Also you can list exceptions for pages where you do not want a module to appear.

## Payment

Select and restrict currency and the way to pay.

# Preferences

Lets you configure and fine-tune some of your store's details:

| Subtabs | Description |
|---|---|
| **General** | Enable your store, multistore, or SSL here. |
| **Orders** | Set up the minimum purchase total required, the order process type, enable guest checkout, and others. |

| Subtabs | Description |
|---|---|
| **Products** | This subtab has loads of options, all to do with products and how they are presented. There's more on this in *Chapter 5, Tools, Newsletters, Extra Income, and Statistics*. |
| **Customers** | Customer-related options, most notably the B2B mode. |
| **Themes** | Enable your theme for your e-commerce. |
| **SEO & URLs** | Enable **Friendly URL** and set up titles and urls for standard page in PrestaShop. |
| **CMS** | This is the PrestaShop Content Management System. It can create and manage all of your articles here. The CMS is covered in *Chapter 4, Getting More Customers*, as well as how to write articles. |
| **Image** | Use these settings to customize the look and feel of your store. This is covered in *Chapter 2, Back Office*. |
| **Store Contacts** | Provides a complete physical store contact information. Obviously, this is only useful if you have a physical store. |
| **Search** | Configure the importance of different factors for PrestaShop search. More information is provided in *Chapter 4, Getting More Customers*. |
| **Maintenance** | Active or deactivate your store on maintenance mode. |
| **Geolocation** | Allows your store to identify customer location. |

# Advanced Parameters

| Subtabs | Description |
|---|---|
| **Configuration Information** | Brief resume about your PrestaShop configuration. |
| **Performance** | Improve your e-commerce performance, by enabling some options here. |
| **E-mail** | Configure or reconfigure all of your e-mail options here. Have a look at *Chapter 5, Tools, Newsletters, Extra Income, and Statistics*, before fiddling with these. |
| **CSV Import** | The CSV import page enables you to easily fill your product catalog when you have a very large amount of product or data from an other e-commerce tool. |
| **DB backup** | Use this quick and simple database backup tool. Full backups are discussed in *Chapter 6, Security and Disaster Recovery*. |
| **SQL Manager** | Explore a database using the SQL language. |
| **Logs** | It is a list of errors in your e-commerce. |
| **Webservice** | You can enable your shop's webservice, so that third-party tools can access your data. |

# Administration

You can do some changes here that impact the front-end and even your business:

| Subtabs | Description |
| --- | --- |
| Preferences | General options and settings for PrestaShop functionality. |
| Quick Accesses | Add and remove areas of your admin control panel that can be accessed via the quick access feature. There's more in *Chapter 5, Tools, Newsletters, Extra Income, and Statistics*. |
| Employees | This tab defines what users can do and who deals with each type of customer contact. |
| Profiles | Creating and assigning profiles for employees using your PrestaShop profile is both useful and makes good sense from a security perspective. Explore this idea more fully in *Chapter 6, Security and Disaster Recovery*. |
| Permissions | Assign permissions to your profiles and specify the amount of access, if any, that each profile has on each of the tabs. This is fully explained in *Chapter 6, Security and Disaster Recovery*. |
| Menus | Sort the way that you want the back-end menu. |

# Stats

The subject of statistics is as wide as it is important. Set up PrestaShop to gather statistics in *Chapter 5, Tools, Newsletters, Extra Income, and Statistics*, learn to interpret statistics in *Chapter 9, Go... to the Future*, and make a plan for using statistics in *Chapter 9, Go... to the Future*.

| Subtabs | Description |
| --- | --- |
| Search Engines | A list of search engines and parameters that PrestaShop is already configured to gather referral statistics for. |
| Referrers | Options for indexing your site's referrers and cleaning the cache of referrer data. |

# B
# Web Resources

*Here are a few web resources to help you build your e-commerce business.*

## PrestaShop related resources

`www.prestashop.com`

The official home of the PrestaShop project, including multi-lingual forum, wiki, and much more.

`www.prestastore.com`

Buy modules and themes for your PrestaShop.

`www.prestabox.com`

Turn-key hosting for PrestaShop.

`www.presto-changeo.com`

Loads of PrestaShop tips, tricks, and cool modules.

## Sales and marketing

`www.warriorforum.com`

A bit hard core but incredible information, advice, and feedback about all things on marketing.

# Technical

`www.smarty.net`

PrestaShop template engine.

`www.php.net`

Want to understand the code that makes PrestaShop run? This is the place to start.

`www.w3schools.com`

Easily the best resource for all things about World Wide Web coding. Just add `/css` to the URL for the best CSS resource bar none.

# Resources

`www.dreamstime.com`

As many images at reasonable prices that you could ever want.

`www.istockphoto.com`

A bit dearer than dreamstime but some really high quality, arty stuff can be found here.

`www.sourceforge.net`

The largest free software site.

# Other shopping carts and content management systems

`www.zen-cart.com`

Another open source shopping cart based in PHP and MySQL.

`www.joomla.org`

A CMS, but can be easily added to the Virtuemart webshop component at
`www.virtuemart.net`.

`www.wordpress.org`

One of the best open source CMS in the market. It is very easy to add a plugin and convert this CMS into a shop. WooCommerce webshop or GetShopped plugins does a good work.

`www.oscommerce.net`

`www.magentocommerce.com`

`www.drupal.org`

`www.cubecart.com`

# Other

`www.businesszone.co.uk`

A general business forum and information site. It deals with all aspects of business but with an inclination towards Internet enterprise.

`http://smallbusinessonlinecommunity.bankofamerica.com/index.jspa`

A great forum for all things on business.

# Pop Quiz Answers

## Chapter 1, Getting Started

### Pop quiz – starting your e-commerce

| Q1 | 2. Enable multistore |
|---|---|
| Q2 | 3. Stats |
| Q3 | 1. Click on Catalog and then click on **Product** |

## Chapter 2, Back Office

### Pop quiz – themes and things

| Q1 | 1. Editing the HTML template with CSS and JavaScript |
|---|---|
| Q2 | 2. Editing the CSS file of the theme |
| Q3 | 1. Click on the Themes sub-tab under Preferences and once there, I select my logo |

## Chapter 3, Merchandising for Success

### Pop quiz – a few product marketing questions

| Q1 | 1. Creating a special offer |
|---|---|
| Q2 | 2. The new body toner uses the latest fitness technology |

# Chapter 4, Getting More Customers

## Pop quiz – PrestaShop search

| Q1 | 2. Setting weight in the section Search under the Preferences tabs |
|----|-------------------------------------------------------------------|
| Q2 | 1. Adding to the file the following line, Disallow: [Path] |

# Chapter 5, Tools, Newsletters, Extra Income, and Statistics

## Pop quiz – tools and preferences challenge

| Q1 | 1. By selecting **Use PHP mail() function. Recommended; works in most cases** |
|----|------------------------------------------------------------------------------|
| Q2 | 2. By clicking on **Menus** under the **Administration** tab |
| Q3 | 1. Yes, PrestaShop does everything for us |

# Chapter 6, Security and Disaster Recovery

## Pop quiz – security

| Q1 | 1. To be consistent with every profile |
|----|-----------------------------------------|
| Q2 | 3. Change the design of our store, add or delete an other employee, modify the orders, among others |
| Q3 | 1. Using SSL |

# Chapter 7, Checkouts and Shipping

## Pop quiz – a refresher

| Q1 | 3. Because it is a protocol for encrypting information over the Internet |
|---|---|
| Q2 | 1. Because, when the customers use the PayPal payment gateway, they automatically jump to the PayPal servers |

# Chapter 8, Ready to Sell

## Pop quiz – sell your products

| Q1 | 1. Forum, specialized webs, search engine registration and AdWords |
|---|---|
| Q2 | 2. Products that the customer often buys |
| Q3 | 1. Having a good SEO, writing good posts and giving a good customer services |

# Chapter 9, Go... to the Future

## Pop quiz – become an e-commerce expert

| Q1 | 1. It is more important to have a very good product line and customer services |
|---|---|
| Q2 | 1. Magento, PrestaShop, and osCommerce |
| Q3 | 2. Audience |

# Index

## E

e-commerce
  about 194
  future 212
e-commerce business
  profitability, increasing 206-211
e-mail list
  accessing 115, 116
e-mail marketing
  about 107
  stages 109
  with newsletters 108
E-mail, Preferences tab 103
e-mail service provider
  for sending newsletters 114
e-mail system
  for sending newsletters 114
E-mail tab 49
employees security 125

## F

FAB technique 62
Facebook 183
features
  about 71
  using 72, 73
feedback
  getting, for products 173-175
files
  backing up 134
  restoring 136
  transferring, to web host 9
friendly URL 84
front page
  discount voucher, putting on 175, 176
FTP 134

## G

General, Preferences tab 102
General subsection, Preferences tab 40
gift wrapping
  setting up 164, 165

GIMP
  images, creating 63
  URL 63
global.css file 45
good posts
  writing 178
Google 81, 177
Google AdSense
  installing 116, 117
  setting up, in PrestaShop 116, 117
Google AdWords 201
Google Analytics
  about 80, 120, 201
  account, obtaining 120
  audience 201-203
  content 203
  installing 120, 121
  traffic sources 203
  URL 120
  using 121
Google Checkout
  about 142, 169
  Bank wire 150
  cash on delivery 149
  cheque orders 149
  installing 147-149
  using 147
Google sitemaps
  tutorial 93
Google Webmaster Tools 177
graph, PrestaShop statistics 118
grid engines, PrestaShop statistics 118
groups
  about 183, 189
  creating 190
  using 190
guest checkout 152

## H

home page
  content, adding to 35-37
  modules, moving 39, 40
  secure payment 38
  USP 34, 35
Home text editor 35

# S

sales taxes **150**
sale value
  shipping, configuring by **160, 161**
**Search Engine Optimization.** *See* **SEO**
**search engines**
  registering with **177**
**search-friendly URLs**
  obtaining **84, 85**
**search weightings, PrestaShop**
  about **93, 94**
  languages conclusion **99**
  languages, switching **96, 97**
  translations, creating **97, 98**
**secure payment 38**
**Secure Sockets Layer.** *See* **SSL**
**security attacks**
  brute force **124**
  common sense issues **124**
  cross-site scripting **124**
  SQL injection attack **124**
  types **124**
  user error **124**
**SEO 80**
**SEO & URLs subsection, Preferences tab 40**
**shared SSL 131**
**shipping**
  about **31, 158, 218**
  calculated by sale value **160**
  configuring, by sale value **160, 161**
  configuring, by weight **161, 162**
  scenarios **159, 160**
**shipping options**
  about **158**
  super-simple shipping configuration
     options **159**
**Shipping tabs**
  Carriers **218**
  Price Ranges **218**
  Weight Ranges **218**
**shop**
  customer account, creating for **50, 51**
**shop-back 22, 23**
**shop categories**
  about **55**
  structure, planning **56**

**shop front 20, 21**
**Shop Importer 54**
**shopping cart module**
  installing **33, 34**
**Shopping Carts tab 190**
**site**
  marketing **177**
**sitemap 93**
**sitemaps.xml file 93**
**social media**
  Facebook **183**
  Twitter **179**
  used, for promoting store **179-184**
**Social Share buttons 178**
**spam 113**
**spamming**
  avoiding **183**
**special offer**
  about **67**
  creating **67**
**SQL injection attack 124**
**SSL**
  about **130**
  setting up, in PrestaShop **132**
  using **143**
**statistics options**
  exploring **119, 120**
**statistics, PrestaShop site**
  analyzing **195-203**
**Stats**
  about **51, 221**
  Referrers **221**
  Search Engines **221**
**statuses 186, 187**
**store**
  contacting **53**
  copy, creating for **132, 133**
  promoting, social media used **179-184**
**Store contacts, Preferences tab 102**
**store logo**
  uploading **48, 49**
**subcategories**
  content, creating for **60**
**subscriber list**
  obtaining **114, 116**
**subscribers**
  list, building **111**

## Thank you for buying
# PrestaShop 1.5 Beginner's Guide

## About Packt Publishing

Packt, pronounced 'packed', published its first book "*Mastering phpMyAdmin for Effective MySQL Management*" in April 2004 and subsequently continued to specialize in publishing highly focused books on specific technologies and solutions.

Our books and publications share the experiences of your fellow IT professionals in adapting and customizing today's systems, applications, and frameworks. Our solution based books give you the knowledge and power to customize the software and technologies you're using to get the job done. Packt books are more specific and less general than the IT books you have seen in the past. Our unique business model allows us to bring you more focused information, giving you more of what you need to know, and less of what you don't.

Packt is a modern, yet unique publishing company, which focuses on producing quality, cutting-edge books for communities of developers, administrators, and newbies alike. For more information, please visit our website: www.packtpub.com.

## About Packt Open Source

In 2010, Packt launched two new brands, Packt Open Source and Packt Enterprise, in order to continue its focus on specialization. This book is part of the Packt Open Source brand, home to books published on software built around Open Source licences, and offering information to anybody from advanced developers to budding web designers. The Open Source brand also runs Packt's Open Source Royalty Scheme, by which Packt gives a royalty to each Open Source project about whose software a book is sold.

## Writing for Packt

We welcome all inquiries from people who are interested in authoring. Book proposals should be sent to author@packtpub.com. If your book idea is still at an early stage and you would like to discuss it first before writing a formal book proposal, contact us; one of our commissioning editors will get in touch with you.

We're not just looking for published authors; if you have strong technical skills but no writing experience, our experienced editors can help you develop a writing career, or simply get some additional reward for your expertise.

open source
community experience distilled

Building eCommerce
Sites with Drupal
Commerce Cookbook

Over 50 recipes to help you build beautiful, responsive
eCommerce sites with Drupal Commerce

Richard Carter          PACKT open source

## Building eCommerce Sites with Drupal Commerce Cookbook

ISBN: 978-1-782161-22-6          Paperback: 226 pages

Over 50 recipes to help you to build beautiful,
responsive eCommerce sites with Drupal Commerce

1. Learn how to build attractive eCommerce sites with
   Drupal Commerce

2. Customise your Drupal Commerce store for
   maximum impact

3. Reviewed by the creators of Drupal Commerce:
   The CommerceGuys

Mastering Magento

Maximize the power of Magento: for developers, designers,
and store owners

Bret Williams          PACKT open source

## Mastering Magento

ISBN: 978-1-849516-94-5          Paperback: 300 pages

Maximize the power of Magneto: for developers,
designers, and store owners

1. Learn how to customize your Magento store for
   maximum performance

2. Exploit little known techniques for extending and
   tuning your Magento installation.

3. Step-by-step guides for making your store run faster,
   better and more productively

Please check **www.PacktPub.com** for information on our titles

open source
community experience distilled

## PrestaShop 1.3 Theming – Beginner's Guide

ISBN: 978-1-849511-72-8 Paperback: 312 pages

Develop flexible, powerful, and proffessional themes for your PrestaShop store through simple steps

1. Control the look and feel of your PrestaShop store by creating customized themes

2. Learn the tips and tricks to make theming in PrestaShop easier

3. Create your own PrestaShop theme in a few simple steps

4. A beginner's guide packed with step-by-step exercises to simplify your task of developing a new theme for PrestaShop stores

## Instant E-Commerce with Magento: Build a Shop

ISBN: 978-1-782164-86-9 Paperback: 52 pages

A fast-paced, practical guide to building your own shop with Magneto

1. Learn something new in an Instant! A short, fast, focused guide delivering immediate results.

2. Learn how to install and configure an online shop with Magento

3. Tackle difficult tasks like payment gateways, shipping options, and custom theming

4. Full of clear screenshots and step-by-step instructions

Please check **www.PacktPub.com** for information on our titles

www.ingramcontent.com/pod-product-compliance
Lightning Source LLC
Chambersburg PA
CBHW060537060326
40690CB00017B/3520